WELCOME

Finding cars in museums I drove on their press launches makes me a veteran of motor reporting. Yet it was surprising at a 1976 preview of the Ford Fiesta to find how much it resembled the 5-year-old Fiat 127 at home in the garage. Here was another boxy two-door hatchback with rectangular headlights, a crosswise engine like a Mini's, and front wheel drive. The Fiat was a bit less trendy, but it looked as though Ford had overdone its research on a small car for Europe and come up with much the same.

It had not. The Fiesta was far better made. The Fiat was rusty, slow, clumsy, and austere. Fiestas rode smoothly, were quieter, comfier and were dearly loved and trusted family members more than 22 million times.

Tens of thousands of British people learned to drive in them. Ford supplied Fiestas to the AA Driving School for 25 years. Fiestas were top seller 12 years in a row, 4.8 million in the UK, 17.8 million in Europe. Ford now supplies the Fiesta's replacement, the Puma, to the AA Driving School. Plus *ça change, plus c'est la meme chose…*

The Fiesta was so successful it went global – such a success in fact, it was reinvented as van, rally car, sports car, small car and even an SUV. Getting on for half a century later, the Fiesta had become a slightly bigger, sleeker ecologically correct replacement. It never really stopped in its tracks. It just changed.

Ford brought motoring to millions in the tween-war years. Plain Prefects, angular Anglias after it was disunited from its first British factory in Manchester and spread its wings to Dagenham and Europe. Ford made Zephyrs and Zodiacs. Ford Europe made a Teutonic Taunus, then from 1972 created Fiestas with a wider scope than the popular Popular, with choices of engines, trims and styles. Every family had one. Every generation. Everybody has been in a Fiesta.

Ford made its final Fiestas in 2023. Generations will still travel in them, still enjoy them, still buy them, still sell them. The Fiesta had magic ingredients. It was the right recipe. It became baked into the motoring psyche.

Eric Dymock
Editor

Repetition. Ford sold Mark 1 Fiestas to the AA Driving School. So many people learned on them that it was natural for the Puma to be their 2020s successor.

ISBN 978 1 80282 745 3
Editor: Eric Dymock
Cover image: Ford Press office
Text revised and adapted from The Ford in Britain File (two editions 2002, 2006) and The Ford in Britain Centenary File (2011) ISBN 978-0-9554909-3-4. Published by Dove Publishing/ copyright Eric Dymock
Senior editor, specials: Roger Mortimer
Email: roger.mortimer@keypublishing.com
Design: Panda Media
Advertising Sales Manager: Brodie Baxter
Email: brodie.baxter@keypublishing.com
Tel: 01780 755131
Advertising Production: Debi McGowan
Email: debi.mcgowan@keypublishing.com

SUBSCRIPTION/MAIL ORDER
Key Publishing Ltd, PO Box 300, Stamford, Lincs, PE9 1NA
Tel: 01780 480404
Subscriptions email: subs@keypublishing.com
Mail Order email: orders@keypublishing.com
Website: www.keypublishing.com/shop

PUBLISHING
Group CEO: Adrian Cox
Publisher, Books and Bookazines: Jonathan Jackson
Published by: Key Publishing Ltd, PO Box 100, Stamford, Lincs, PE9 1XQ
Tel: 01780 755131
Website: www.keypublishing.com

PRINTING
Precision Colour Printing Ltd, Haldane, Halesfield 1, Telford, Shropshire. TF7 4QQ

DISTRIBUTION
Seymour Distribution Ltd, 2 Poultry Avenue, London, EC1A 9PU
Enquiries Line: 02074 294000.

CONTENTS

American Model T: Any colour so long as it's black.

Henry Ford 2 and Fiesta 1.

BOBCAT
FIESTA ONE

Car makers always wanted to invent one model, make it cheap and sell it to the world. Ford did so with the Model T – one design, one formula, unchanging. 'Tin Lizzie' sold 15 million before 1927. The Fiesta sold more but took twice as long, and was changed seven times. A modern-market adaptable, it appealed to city-dwellers as well as young audience on the lookout for a hot hatch. Ford made the Fiesta in 12 countries, sold it in 50. Model Ts famously were any colour so long as it was black, Fiestas were multi-coloured, multi-purpose. Model Ts had integral engines, an epicyclic gearbox (needs explanation) and three pedals. The middle one engaged reverse, the left pedal engaged low gears when pressed, high gears when released. The one on the right was a transmission brake. A lever on the steering column controlled engine speed, transverse springs meant it only had two - one front, one back – it was cheap and easy to make – seven an hour on the world's first moving car assembly line.

Model Ts came from America, then, from 1911 the former country seat of Sir Humphrey

de Trafford. Two legs of the Bridgewater Canal made his Trafford Park almost an island, so the good lord sold out. After 1896 it was an industrial site for Manchester. Henry Ford leased a former tramcar factory, shipped T-bits over the Atlantic and the Ship Canal and for a time his strictures about paintwork were set aside. Manchester Model Ts got three coats, blue, later green with black mudguards then brown for 1914.

Back in Detroit Henry disapproved. Post-war all Ts were black.

You could never disavow Ford family strictures. The origin of the Fiesta came in June 1967 when Henry Ford II decided to bring Ford of Britain and Ford Werke of Germany together. Top floor executives in Dearborn created Ford of Europe. Dagenham and Cologne had been separate until that point. They had already disagreed over a middle-class car, codenamed in Germany as the Cardinal. Ford Britain with a show of seniority, called it the Archbishop.

Henry II thought Cortina and Taunus unnecessarily different, it was wasteful,

so he knocked heads together: "There's only one Volkswagen in Europe, only one Renault, only one Fiat. We should have only one Ford." He amalgamated them and told them the Escort, then under development, had to be the same for both. Introduced in 1968, the Escort was made at Saarlouis in Germany and Ford's Halewood factory in the North-West of England.

Then it was decided on 3 December 1973 to make something smaller than the Escort. The world was changing. Cars were downsizing. Following the first oil crisis after a Middle Eastern war, the Organisation of Arab Petroleum Exporting Countries (OAPEC) imposed an embargo. Oil prices trebled; the industrial world trembled as gas-guzzling cars became history. It was not so much an environmental issue as economic, that came later. Put plainly, buyers were going to buy fewer big cars, so the industry had to have a plan.

Committees of experts predicted trends, watched share prices, governments, taxation trends, read the commentaries on world affairs

Ford Germany's 1950's Taunus.

and advised that wealthy elite on the top floor in Dearborn. Like so many global calamities, it was difficult to forecast. A lot of guesswork described options following a decade that had begun with conspicuous consumption. Thoughtless exploitation of the world's resources was not yet a big issue. What came to be known as global warming or climate change was no more than a cloud on the horizon. However, simply as an issue of global good housekeeping, motoring behemoths were becoming unfashionable, unsustainable. Smaller cars had to be ready.

Ever since the Suez crisis of the 1950s prompted the Mini, Ford project teams had been looking at it. They had taken Minis to pieces, analysed every nut, bolt and screw, concluding that the British Motor Corporation was losing money on every one. Ford had some of the best accountant analysts in the industry and they were right. Mini cars made mini profits because they cost about the same to make as big cars and could never be sold at premium prices. Miniature cars had to have miniature prices, yet they needed the same number of people to build, used the same tooling, suffered the same overheads, paid the same taxes and as Ford's bean-counters found, the sums didn't add up.

Ford knew exactly what components cost whether made in house or bought elsewhere. Saving a few pounds on the amount of sheet steel a small car needed was trifling. Small wheels and tyres cost nearly as much as big ones. Advertising, dealer discounts and marketing were all considered as Ford carefully stripped down 30 cars including Renault 5s, Honda Civics, Toyotas and Datsuns. A hundred and thirty engineer-accountant teams set price and weight targets they could apply to themselves, to a small Ford.

Dearborn-ers had never quite got over the worldwide success of the Model T. They still wanted to make a world car; one model that could be built in big numbers anywhere. Here, by the oil-thirsty Seventies they saw an opportunity.

Governments everywhere were backing projects to create jobs. Spain was expanding its industrial base to prepare for entry to the Common Market as it was still called and in 1974 subsidised a new plant at Valencia. Ford seized the chance to make a sub-Escort class car for Europe now, maybe the world later. It was codenamed Bobcat and a billion dollars set aside for design, development, and production, the team coming under Trevor Erskine. It would not be the smallest Ford, but targets were set for it to cost $100 less to make and be shorter than an Escort. Its style would be drawn up by Tom Tjaarda at the newly established Ghia centre in Turin under the direction of Ford Europe's director Uwe Bahnsen.

The oil crises brought things to a head and on 18 October 1976, Henry Ford 2, together with King Juan Carlos opened the

Ford Britain 1960's Cortina 1 engineered like King George V.

new Valencia plant, which was soon making engines. The plan was for the new sub-compact to use transaxles from a transmissions plant at Bordeaux and other bits from Eire, Britain, and Germany. Lots of names for Bobcat had been suggested and Mr Ford encouraged something Spanish, opting for "Fiesta" meaning "party". It had been used once for an Oldsmobile but as a real word it could scarcely be challenged. It was alliterative with "Ford", so Fiesta it was and Valencia planned to make 500,000 a year in conjunction with Saarlouis, Germany, and Dagenham, UK.

The European sub-compact market was dominated by Renault 5, Volkswagen Golf, and Fiat 127; Ford had not made one from

scratch like this since the Model Y in 1934 and adopted the successful Fiat as a role model. It had been decided Bobcat would be a bit longer. Like all the other rivals, 127s had been dissected and examined, so Ford researchers chopped their bodies off and used their platforms as a basis. The Fiesta's conception, and even its styling in Turin studios, owed much to the Fiat 127, which was not uniques. Car manufacturers had been doing it for generations – it wasn't copying, it was inspiration. Ford not only used the Fiat as a basis for comparison but some of its prototypes were shamelessly constructed on 127 underpinnings.

Outsiders were invited for secret assessments, experimental unbadged Fiestas

Clay modelling began in 1974.

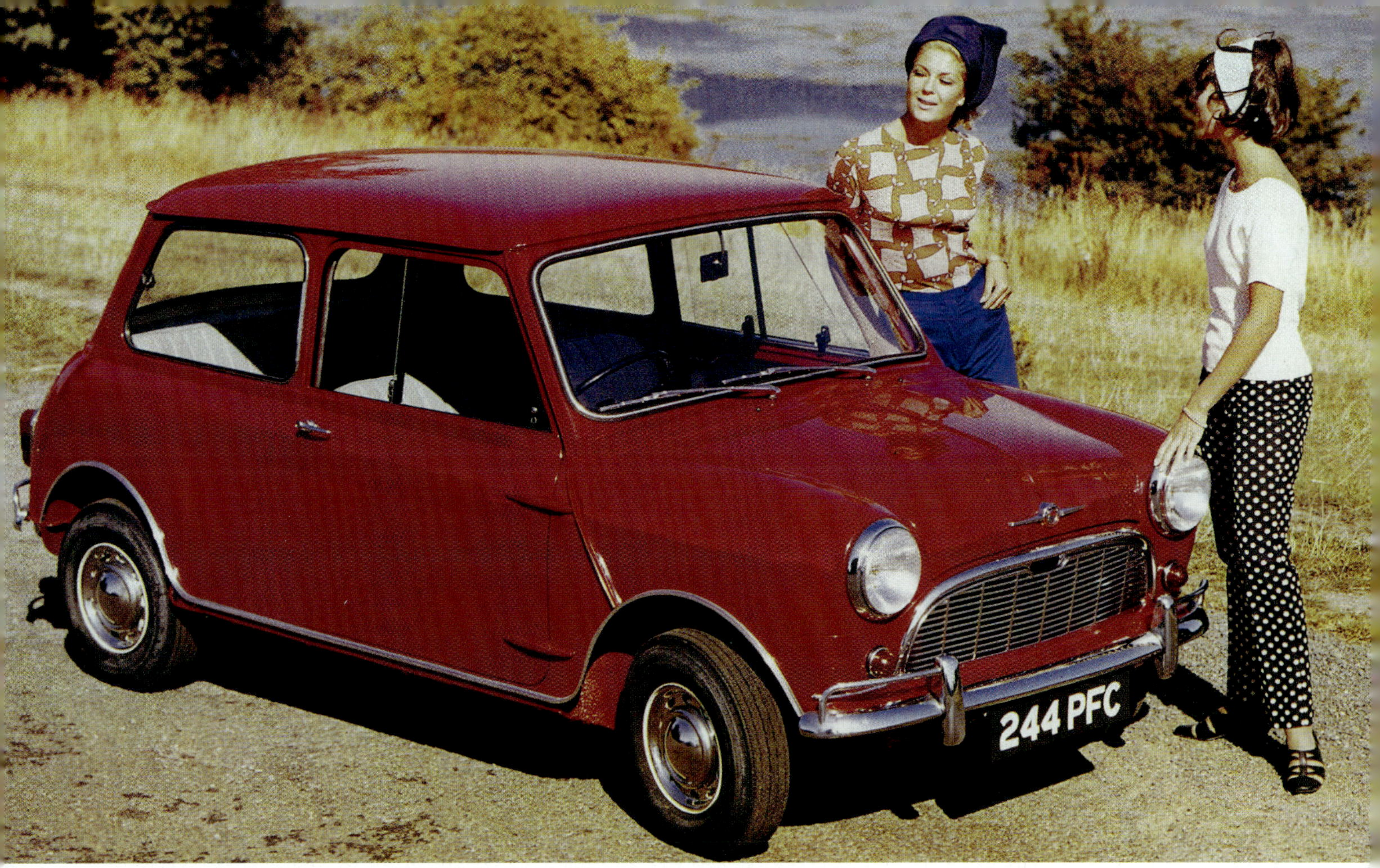

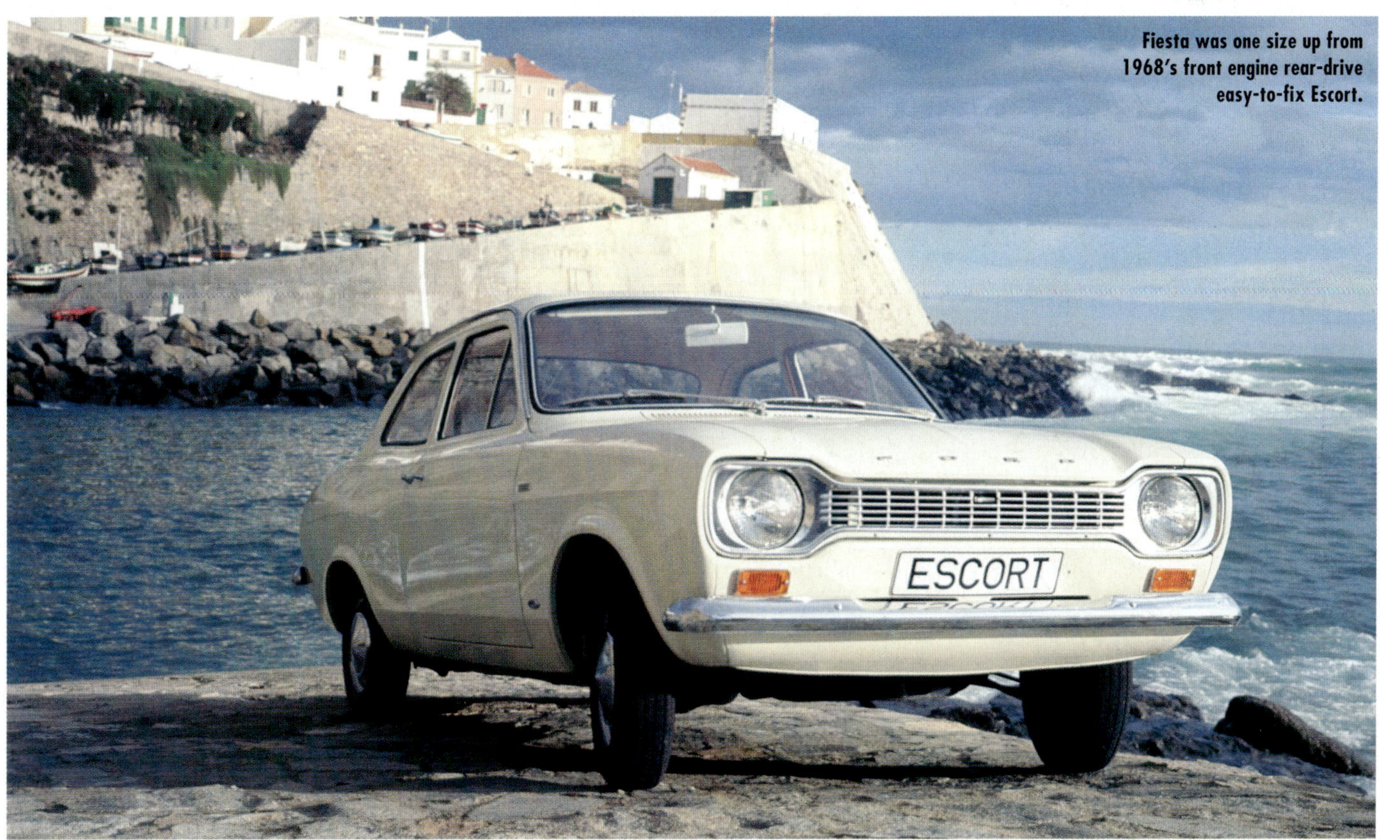

Ford accountants disparaged BMC's Mini: its engineers learned lessons.

were lined up beside the Peugeot 104, Honda Civic, Renault 5, as well as the Fiat. Guests flown to Lausanne were not told what make the mystery cars were. They were given questionnaires and, in some of the answers, Fiats and still-secret Fiestas ran neck and neck. At a similar clinic in California 700 people signalling support for front wheel drive, filed past them together with a Volkswagen Beetle and Ford Pinto.

Tasked with developing the Fiesta for production, engineers worked on five principal patterns. Four were composites on Fiat 127s, modified to carry one Ford-designed sub assembly. These included a front suspension, engine and transmission, or an electrical system. One was almost entirely Ford. They were assessed always against the Fiat, tests were carried out on a gearshift, to see if it could have smoother movement and crucially to see if it could be made cheaper. The accountants calculated Fiesta could be made for $100.36 less than an Escort, it could be 11 per cent cheaper and 245lb (111.1kg) lighter, although frustratingly turned out 17lb (7.7kg) heavier than the Fiat. It would have only 2,943 separate components against the Escort's 4,077. Fiat made 3,730,000 127s, stopping only in 1983 just as the second-generation Fiesta began.

Fiesta was one size up from 1968's front engine rear-drive easy-to-fix Escort.

There had been dozens of body styles, so it was all the more surprising when the final shape was decided by the assembled top executive committee on 2 October 1973, that it still looked like a Fiat. Clinics were held in Düsseldorf, Paris, Milan, and Madrid, the Fiesta gaining over convenience, a nicer interior, and better visibility. It was certainly better to drive, had a smoother ride and was nimbler.

Some public previews were subtle. In 1975 a Fiesta went on display to crowds at the Le Mans 24 Hours' race. Carefully arranged spy shots appeared before the first Fiestas went on sale in France and Germany in September 1975. UK dealers had to wait until January 1977 for the first right hand drive cars. It was the smallest-engined Ford since the 1950s Dagenham Anglias and Prefects, that had been developed in the 1930s.

The Fiesta still exemplified engineering caution. Ever since the Model T, Ford Motor Company's policy was to continue with designs and components for as long as it could. It had only reluctantly dispensed with separate chassis frames; it preferred as little change as possible. Side-valve engines, three-speed gearboxes, cart-type springing of those Dagenham relics all lasted into the 1960s. The 100E Popular barely exceeded 70mph, so by comparison the Fiesta was radical and quick. Turning the engine sideways and driving the front wheels, inescapably followed the logic of Alec Issigonis's Mini. He boxed up the engine and transmission at the front, leaving more space for passengers. It was cheap to build, and customers loved it notwithstanding what Ford's astute accountants had discovered.

Head of Ford design Uwe Bahnsen 1975.

Ford was at last compelled to abandon side-valves. Fiesta came with the Valencia 957cc (with high and low-compression options for different markets) and a 1117cc unit essentially a cut-down crossflow Kent inherited from the 105E Anglia of 1959. There was still a legacy of the transfer machinery on which they were produced – new production equipment would have been costly. It was how Ford kept costs under control. Kents kept the same spaces between the cylinders and, up until now, a cylinder bore of 81mm whatever their stroke. It was such parsimony or clever accounting and making best use of machine toolrooms that dictated engine dimensions and capacity. Fiesta Kents were shrunk with 74mm bores, a shorter block and a shorter crankshaft that managed perfectly well on three main bearings rather than a smoother-running five.

Henry Ford and King Juan Carlos open 2.7 million square metre factory.

Ford dealers had to learn about transverse engines in Fiestas.

Anglia 100E 1953-1959, side valves, three gears, Lulworth Cove.

The strokes selected now were 55.7mm, giving a capacity of 957cc, and 65mm, giving 1117cc. It was not until 1977 that the engineering work (and expensive new tooling) achieved a five main bearing 1300 engine.

Introducing a new car was elaborate. Ford dealers' involvement was vital but unfamiliarity with the transverse engine-transmission unitary structure worried them. They would no longer be able to change a faulty clutch without removing the engine and gearbox. Keeping service and repair costs down was important in view of the still-important fleet market. Many small capacity working-class cars were bought by commercial fleets for salesmen, reps, and small businesspeople and they were worried too.

Ford had managed to keep the price of the Fiesta close to the best-selling cars in their class and overall cost of ownership mattered. Ford claimed routine service costs had been cut by a quarter and dealers 'technicians underwent introduction courses at Ford's Service Training Colleges, with the UK's

being in Daventry. Fiesta service intervals were kept at an industry average of 6000 miles or 12 months. Low insurance costs were expected with the help of plastic bumpers that resisted knocks. Front wings were bolted on rather than welded. Generous apertures inside the body shell allowed access to panels damaged in accidents. The designers had provided places where they could be repaired with part-panels – small pieces instead of expensive main parts.

Fiestas were carefully detailed to simplify or even sometimes eliminate servicing. Door locks and hinges were lubricated for life, along with wheel bearings and the handbrake cable. Clutch and handbrake were self-adjusting. The old problem of replacing worn clutches could be achieved without totally dismantling a car. Breakerless electronic ignition completely did away with the distributor so that there was nothing mechanical to wear or put out of adjustment. The only ignition parts that needed changing regularly were the spark plugs.

Once the Fiesta got into its stride, changes were made to engine and gearbox mountings, there was a bigger radiator and a higher-ratio final drive. The 1300 was given a thicker anti-roll bar, stiffer springs, adjustable dampers, and trendy (for a time at any rate) striped upholstery rather like deckchairs. The alternative was a Ghia version (Ford had already bought into Italian design studios) with better all-round comfort, luxury trim and laminated instead of toughened glass windscreens. Both models had 155SR-12 tyres and when the 5-bearing engine arrived it put the weight up to 885kg (1951lb). Maximum speed was 151kph (94.1mph); 0-100kph (62mph) 13.7sec, fuel consumption 8.9l/100km (31.7mpg) and the 1300S cost £2844.

On 11 May 1976, the first of 84,00 Fiestas to be built at Saarlouis that year, rolled off the production line. They would be made at Valencia and in 1977 at Dagenham, still with transmissions from Bordeaux, cylinder blocks and radiators from

Fiesta 1, 1976 Fiesta, 957cc/1117cc.

England, carburettors from Belfast, brought together in an elaborate logistical system that took time to arrange. It quickly became Europe's fastest-selling car, half a million in the first year, three million by face-lift time to 1984 Fiesta II. Saarlouis cars were slightly different for export to America; they were Base, Décor, Sport, and Ghia with the best trim. They also had a catalytic converter for California's emission regulations, so they had a more powerful 1596cc engine.

Fiestas remained 3-door hatchbacks until 1989, and there was no automatic gearbox option. The design brief had been strict, a 228.6cm (90in) wheelbase, 7.6cm (3in) longer than Fiat 127, and 11.4cm (4.5in) shorter than an Escort, which had been planned in the 1960s and was already in its eighth year of production.

The Fiesta's target weight had been 700kg (1543.2lb) although it came out at 730kg (1609.4lb) when it went on sale in most of Europe in 1976. There were no right-hand drive cars until February 1977, being offered in base, S, and Ghia configurations. A special edition in 1978 coincided with the 75th anniversary of Ford Motor Company.

Spain, perhaps unsurprisingly in view of what it now meant to the Spanish economy, elected the Fiesta as its Car of the Year. In Britain it won the Design Council Efficiency Award. The following year the millionth Fiesta was built along with Saarlouis's two millionth in 1981. The numbers kept mounting through the first three years. Trim levels changed very little, however, improvements to energy-absorbing bumpers,

side-marker lamps, and accident dynamics mostly in response to increasing demands by legislators were added. It even gained optional air conditioning.

Specifications: 4-cylinders, transverse; front; 74mm x 55.7mm, 957cc; compr 9.0:1; comp 8.3:1; 29.8kW (40bhp) @ 6000rpm); 33.6kW (45bhp) @ 6000rpm; 35kW (47bhp)/l; 65Nm (47.7lbft) @ 3000rpm. 1.1: 74 x 65mm; 1117cc; 39.52kW (53bhp) @ 6000rpm; 35.4kW (47.4bhp)/l; 80Nm (59lbft); pushrod ohv; chain-driven camshaft; cast iron cylinder head, block; Ford sonic idle carburettor, mechanical fuel pump; 3-bearing crankshaft. Front wheel drive; 16.5cm (6.5in) sdp clutch; 4-speed synchromesh gearbox; final drive helical spur, 957cc 4.29:1; 1117cc 4.056:1. Steel monocoque structure; independent front suspension by MacPherson struts, coil springs; rear suspension dead axle, trailing links, Panhard rod; telescopic dampers; hydraulic, vacuum servo 22cm (8.7in) front disc brakes; rear drums 17.8cm (7.0in); rack and pinion steering; 34l (7.5 gal) fuel tank; Michelin ZX radial-ply 135-12 or 145-12 tyres. Pvc upholstery, cloth on Ghia, carpets, laminated windscreen. Maximum speed 957cc 126.8kph (79mph), 1117cc 138kph (86mph) Autocar; 24kph (15mph) or 24.9kph (15.5mph) @ 1000rpm; 0-100kph (62mph) 19.6sec or 15.7sec; 21.7kg/kW (16.2kg/bhp); fuel consumption 8l/100km (35.3mpg) or 8.4l/100km (33.6mpg). Starting price at introduction £1856, Fiesta L £2079, Ghia £2657; 1.1L £2179, 1.1 Ghia £2757.

Main: Special edition Fiestas arrived thick and fast.
1979 Sandpiper.
Image far left: Fiesta customized with deckchair seats.

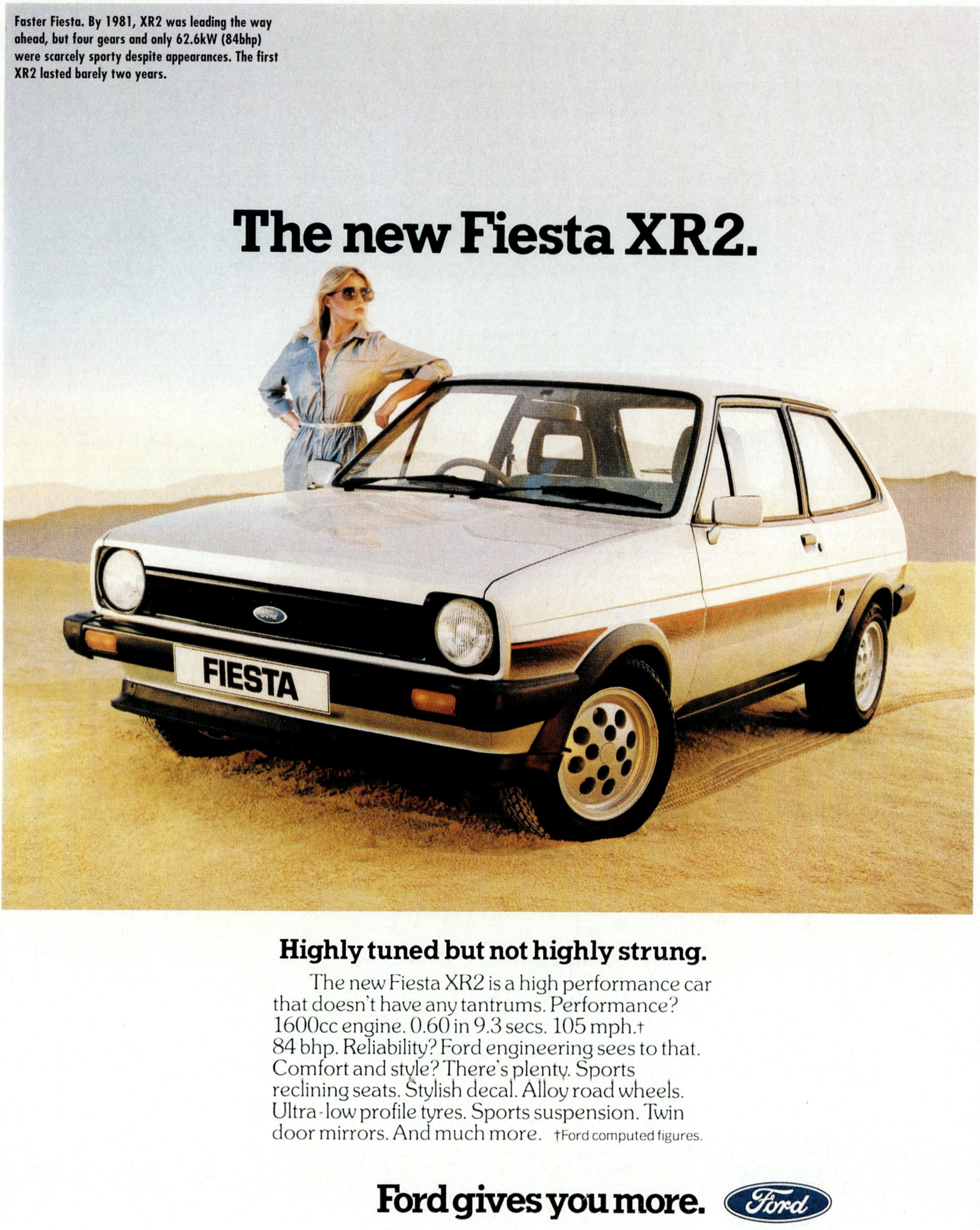
The new Fiesta XR2.
FIESTA
Highly tuned but not highly strung.
The new Fiesta XR2 is a high performance car that doesn't have any tantrums. Performance? 1600cc engine. 0.60 in 9.3 secs. 105 mph.† 84 bhp. Reliability? Ford engineering sees to that. Comfort and style? There's plenty. Sports reclining seats. Stylish decal. Alloy road wheels. Ultra-low profile tyres. Sports suspension. Twin door mirrors. And much more. †Ford computed figures.
Ford gives you more.
Ford

Faster Fiesta. By 1981, XR2 was leading the way ahead, but four gears and only 62.6kW (84bhp) were scarcely sporty despite appearances. The first XR2 lasted barely two years.

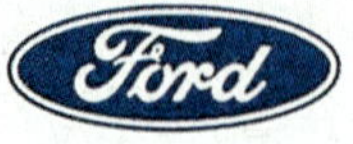

Ford was back in Spain. It hadn't made
a new small car since the Model Y
Miss Spain endorsed in 1932.

Ford was already well into motorsport. It
had beaten Ferrari at Le Mans with the GT40
and won Formula 1 World Championships
with the inspired Cosworth DFV. With Escorts
being rally winners, Cortinas a sporting
flagship, a 1.3 litre Supersport Fiesta
was introduced for the Model Year 1980,
sporting a 1297cc crossflow Kent engine. It
had racy-looking black plastic trim (racing
and rally drivers preferred practicality to
picturesque) and the small square headlights
were replaced by bigger round ones. A
further offshoot was the Fiesta Tuareg off-
road concept, described as "designed and
equipped for practical off-road recreational
use." A Sports Utility Vehicle co-designed with
Ghia was not far off.

Special Vehicle Engineering, set up at
Dunton, turned its attention to the first 100mph
Fiesta. Based on the 1300S, with a 1.6-litre
Kent engine and stiffened suspension, the
XR2 was introduced in September 1981
following a series of Fiesta-only races, set
up in 1979 by Ford's favourite ambassador
Jackie Stewart, with the Faberge Fiesta Ladies
Challenge Series being one example. The
Competitions Department at Boreham set up
to support private rally and racing teams,
prepared a Group B competition version,
supplying and designing X-pack parts kits.

The 1.6 engine was already successful in
North America. It was a combination of the
Federal US specification bottom end and
a 1600GT cylinder head and camshaft,
with a 32/34 DFTA Weber carburettor on
a 1300-pattern (but bigger bore) manifold.
The exhaust was a unique four-into-two cast
iron arrangement. Novel breakerless ignition
exemplified the trend towards increasing
electronics for engine management and with
9.0:1 compression it gave 62kW (83.1bhp)
@ 5500rpm; 38.8kW (52bhp)/l; 125Nm
(92lbft) @ 5500rpm and was already being
used in Mark II Cortinas and Escorts.

The XR2 gearbox was an Escort pattern,
and the perforated aluminium alloy wheels
were Wolfrace Sonics like those of the 2.8i
Capri, but an inch narrower. 1300S spring
rates were retained with the same anti-roll
bar at the back, and the ride height lowered
by an inch at the front by altering the spring
pan on the MacPherson strut. The tie bar to
the front frame was also lowered to reduce
rearwards pitch on acceleration, not so much
for occupant comfort as to lessen changes
in driveshaft angles that created torque
steer – a nuisance with lightly laden powerful
front wheel drive cars. Yet with still only four
gears, it was scarcely a sporty car despite
appearances. Ford

XR2: Produced 1981-1983. Saloon;
3-doors, 5-seats; weight 800kg (1763.7lb).
4-cylinders, front; transverse; 80.98mm x
77.62mm, 1599cc; compr 9.0:1; 62kW
(83.1bhp) @ 5500rpm; 38.8kW (52bhp)/l;
125Nm (92lbft) @ 5500rpm. Kent; pushrod,
chain-driven camshaft; 2 valves; cast iron
cylinder head and block; Weber 34DFTA
carburettor, transistorised ignition; 5-bearing
crankshaft. Front wheel drive; sdp clutch;
gearbox 4-speed synchromesh; final drive
3.58:1.Steel monocoque structure; ifs by
MacPherson struts, coil springs; anti-roll bar;
rear suspension dead axle, trailing links,
Panhard rod; telescopic dampers; hydraulic,
vacuum servo 24.7cm (9.7in) front disc
brakes; rear drums 17.8cm (7in); rack
and pinion steering; 34l (7.5 gal) fuel tank;
185/60HR 13 tyres; aluminium alloy wheels,
6J rims. Wheelbase 228.6cm (90in); track
133.5cm (52.6in) front, 132cm (52in) rear;
length 356.5cm (140.4in); width 156.5cm
(61.6in); height 136cm (53.5in);
ground clearance 14cm (5.5in); turning
circle 9.45m (31ft). Maximum speed
170kph (105.9mph); 29.7kph (18.5mph)
@ 1000rpm; 0-100kph (62mph) 10.1sec;
12.8kg/kW (9.6kg/bhp); fuel consumption
8.6l/100km (32.9mpg). £5150.

FIESTAS WITH FINESSE
FIESTAS II AND III

Following six years as best-seller in its class in Britain and Germany, August 1983 to 1989, second thoughts for the Fiesta brought more choice, a diesel engine, and a not entirely successful automatic transmission. Ford might have been forgiven for pressing on with none of these since the car was selling so well. Special editions such as the Fiesta Finesse ran to 12,000; over 300,000 specials were built in Britain alone.

Full of confidence Ford began driving the Fiesta up-market, the pricier Fiesta II facelift designed jointly with partner Mazda was in search of Ford's global car ambition. It gained a less erect front end, in the interests of slipperier aerodynamics, despite adding slightly to overall length of 365cm (143.7in). The alterations, which made it resemble the Mazda Festiva, shown at a Tokyo Motor Show, as well as being on sale in the United States, were not purely cosmetic. They had become necessary to provide space for the extra length of the proposed CVH engine and 5-speed transaxle. The shape of the A-pillars was much the same, but the changes provided a marginal slipstream improvement through smoother lines at the front corners, always so critical for smooth airflow. The facelift gained recognition in Cologne, the Fiesta was elevated as a work of art as the Goldener Vogel (golden bird) on top of the tower of the city museum, a creation of action artist HA Schult.

Dealers' Technician courses were updated on the differences between old and new Fiestas. They had to be appraised of sometimes subtle changes to engine, front and rear suspension, ignition and fuel systems, steering, optional anti-lock brakes and new

The 1983 Fiesta II, rounded-off styling, less Fiat-like, 957cc 1117cc.

seats. Ford was particularly proud of their construction with the cloth covering material bonded to the foam cushion inner. That eliminated stitching, loose clips and wires and was also claimed to avoid wrinkles, squeaks, and rattles. New cushions could be fitted in place of any damaged through cigarette burns or stains.

Petrol Fiestas could be adapted to run on unleaded fuel, increasingly demanded by campaigners and legislatures, through simple adjustments to the electronic ignition control. Up-market Fiestas were now sophisticated

with computers managing the engine. Older mechanics and amateur DIY owners, a dying breed perhaps, distrusted sealed electronic boxes. They looked for reassurance that there were simple ways of diagnosing faults without a dealer's electronic fault checking equipment. They did not always find it.

There were already four million Fiestas and they were consistently best-sellers, among the top five in the UK, second-placed only to the Escort in 1986, outselling both the Metro and Vauxhall Nova put together. Although, it did not gain the same popularity in the rest

of Europe, where it languished eighth behind Peugeot 205 and Renault 5 at 363,000. Ford's sights were firmly on VW Golf's million.

Strenuous demands for fuel economy were becoming a national obsession. In the 1980s petrol in Britain passed £0.22 a litre (£1 a gallon), then doubled within the year. Ford ran a Fuel Economy Research Vehicle (FERV), together with much laboratory work, to evaluate engines with 11 different sorts of inlet ports and three shapes of combustion chamber. The result for Fiestas were new cylinder heads with smaller-section inlet ports and smaller

Fiesta Finesse: Ford liked alliteration – especially anything with Fs.

valves, that improved cylinder swirl to give better combustion and increased compression. New cam profiles and an exhaust system that kept the flow from adjoining cylinders apart to reduce back pressure bettered consumption by 18-22 per cent at 75mph and 11-34 per cent on the urban cycle under now mandatory official figures.

Overdrive fifth gear, standard on the new diesel and an optional extra on the 1100, was timely and running 13in tyres at 2.67kg-cm (38psi) front and 2.88kg-cm (41psi) rear to lower rolling resistance as FERV demonstrated with the Escort. Their harsher ride was countered by a more compliant bush for the front suspension tie rod, claimed to give a 2.5 per cent improvement in economy. Among the suspension and steering changes were non-stiction top mounts for the front struts, a 3.3cm (1.3in) wider track, and revised rack and pinion steering.

Further gains in economy were coming despite the emission laws being introduced. These could be contentious, the challenge was how to achieve reductions in carbon monoxide (CO) and oxides of nitrogen (Nox). The choice lay between trying to make the combustion process more complete before the exhaust left the engine, or else cleaning it up afterwards by means of catalytic converters. Ford advocated the former, an elegant solution so in pursuit of it developed CVH or Compound Valve angle Hemispherical chamber technology.

Cars with catalytic converters were obliged to run on an air/fuel mixture of 14.7:1, otherwise their cleansing processes failed. This stoichiometric ratio, as it was known, was critical, but unfortunately was also responsible

Boring at Boreham. Experiments on the old aerodrome perimeter track with an Escort 1300 on hard Pirellis gave 119.7mpg.

1983 Ghia moved Fiestas up-market.

for catalytic converter-equipped cars using more fuel. In 1986 Ford addressed the difficulty, redesigned the CVH's combustion chambers and piston crowns to promote complete combustion, allowing stoichiometric ratios of 17 or 18:1, so less fuel could be used. The resulting Fiesta did 5.4l/100km (52.3mpg) at 90kph (56mph), and 6.8l/100km (41.5mpg) at 120kph (75mph). Power went up roughly nine per cent, using low-friction piston rings and a sequential carburettor with a manual choke.

It was, alas, to no avail. Legislators in Europe and America failed to take account of the technical subtlety, believing lobbyists in favour for catalytic converters, resulting in carburettors being abandoned. The future was surely electronic engine management and as a result of the pressures of legislation, thirstier Fiestas were obliged to have a bigger 40l (8.8 gal) fuel tank.

After three years the 1297cc Fiesta engine was replaced in 1986 by the clever "lean burn" 77.24 x 74.3mm 1392cc with 9.5:1 compression. It had been a brave and under-rated initiative showing there were better ways to defeat exhaust emissions than catalytic converters. So, while Ford may have looked faint-hearted when the 1982 Sierra came out with rear wheel drive, a lively 1.3 engine and the 1.4 with Compound Valve Hemispherical (CVH) overhead cams, hydraulic tappets, maintained Fiesta's technical reputation.

The Fiesta II also had a different facia and trim on lower-spec versions and the whole range extra crushable material to meet ever more demanding legislation on crash impact tests. Two improved Valencia

1986 1.4 CVH engine. Enclosed belt drives overhead camshaft.

engines gained little in power, but achieved a small improvement in torque and new 5-speed gearboxes permitted still higher overall gearing. The suspension was revised to accommodate higher-pressure 13in instead of 12in tyres.

Ford took its time over a diesel Fiesta, waiting until it felt quite certain that demand was going to be sustained and governments were not going to turn back on their taxation policies. Officialdom had been actively encouraging diesel as a key ingredient of good national housekeeping since the lower diesel fraction of oil that came out of the ground seemed better value than the more refined spirit fractions at the top.

In 1981 Ford embarked on a joint research programme with Klockner-Humboldt-Deutz AG, German van and lorry manufacturers. It had been waiting for diesel car sales to pass five per cent as a trigger for production in the European market. It also delayed until it had production machinery left over from the conclusion of the Kent engine programme. Its new 1.6-litre diesel was first employed on the Escort and Orion, remaining a Ford mainstay until the turn of the century. When the Escort and Orion diesels were increased from 1608cc to 1753cc in the autumn of 1988, the Fiesta's, due to be phased out soon afterwards, remained as it was.

UK DIESEL CAR MARKET, THE TOP TEN

Position	Make/Model	Sales	Per cent of diesel car market
1	Citroen BX	15,872	12.7
2	Peugeot 405	12,819	10.4
3	Ford Escort	11,722	9.5
4	Peugeot 205	11,559	9.4
5	Peugeot 309	7,442	6.0
6	Ford Orion	7,378	6.0
7	Vauxhall Astra	6,295	5.0
8	Montego	6,198	5.0
9	Ford Sierra	5,791	4.7
10	Ford Fiesta	4,940	4.0

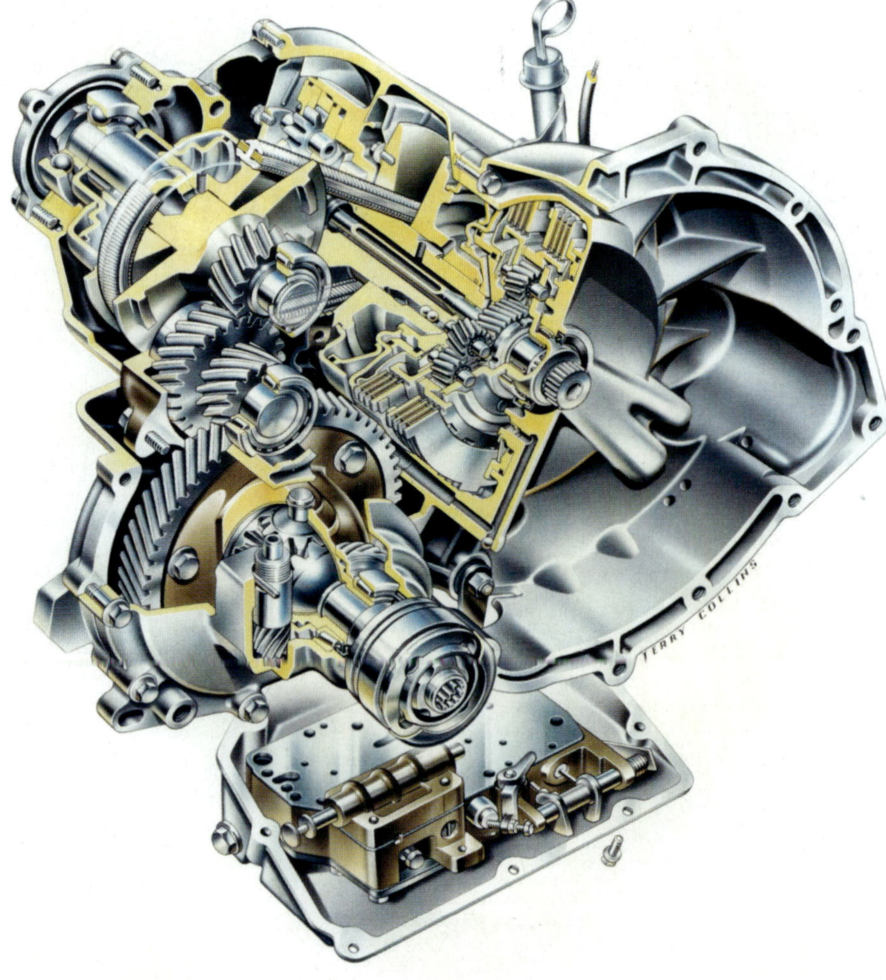

By 1984 Ford advertising of XR2 was lyrical.

Inline Colour O&M. Ford.Fiesta XR2. Autocar. ICS32215   1st Proof

Previewed in May 1983 the Fiesta II diesel engine had an overhead camshaft, was cast iron throughout, and was on hydraulic mountings to reduce body resonance. Apart from the cylinder spacing there were no other hand-me-downs. It had conventional indirect fuel injection; a combination gear and toothed belt drive to the overhead camshaft, and slightly offset in-line vertical valves. One anomaly was that with both bore and stroke at 80mm, it had a swept capacity of 1608.5cc. However according to its German type-approval papers this could still be between 1606.5 and 1611.7 depending on 1mm machining tolerances.

Later in the decade, diesels accounted for one new car in twenty and in Britain the numbers were still going up. In 1988 101,000 rose to over 123,000 despite the rise in the cost of what was still often called DERV, a name derived from an old military term (Diesel Engined Road Vehicles, fuel for the use of). A World Health Authority report, however, highlighting air pollution, created demands for environmentally cleaner diesels. They still had problems with particle emissions, yet governments carried on encouraging them fiscally.

PSA, Peugeot-Citroen, dominated the British diesel car market with the smoothest-running, and some of the liveliest small-capacity engines. Peugeot was eclipsing pioneers such as Mercedes-Benz, which had a production diesel car, the 260D, in 1935. Volkswagen dieselised its Golf successfully in 1974, in the wake of the first oil crisis, but Citroen led the market by a comfortable margin, with the BX taking almost 14 per cent of the segment.

Ford CVT Transaxle laid bare. How Ford squeezed a steel belt into a small space. Segmented steel belt is at top left of Terry Collins's cutaway.

Gas-guzzling Z-cars were a memory. By the 1980s Police were looking for economical Fiestas

Ford was competing against the Vauxhall Astra and the Montego's notably smooth-running Perkins direct-injection engine. The small Fiesta was relatively slow with a top speed of barely 90mph, and sluggish (0 to 60mph in 17.3 seconds), as well as being noisy. Its chief claim to fame was as one of the most economical of all, capable of 54-58mpg.

Fiesta diesels weighed in at 835kg (1840.8lb), the 4-cylinder engine had a compression ratio of 21.5:1, gave 39.5kW (53bhp) @ 4800rpm, a belt-driven overhead camshaft and 5-bearing crankshaft. The 1.6L started out at £6002.

Widening the Fiesta's appeal to drivers wanting more speed, provided the 1984 XR2 with the five gears sporting drivers demanded, together with a 71.6kW (96bhp) 1597cc version of the CVH engine borrowed from the Escort XR3. Low-profile tyres, bigger brakes, stiffer springs and gas-filled dampers, a rear anti-roll bar, wheelarch extensions in smart black plastic and quasi-aerodynamic trappings round the rear window provided further sporting ingredients, although it was still a relatively mildly powered engine since it never wanted to compete seriously with stable-mate, the Escort, which had already graduated to fuel injection.

Fiestas in the meantime, stuck to a simpler and cheaper Weber twin-choke downdraught carburettor. It still needed the special inlet manifold to ensure everything fitted within the small transverse space. The aluminium cylinder head with valves inclined at 45deg and skewed in relation to one another by 7deg gave the complex valve angles of the Compound Valve angle Hemispherical chamber (CVH) title. These

provided a near-hemispherical combustion chamber, representing a triumph of Ford minimalism, working the valves through a single overhead camshaft, spun by a toothed belt. Inclined valves customarily had to be operated by two cams, or a complicated system of rockers, but the 7deg inclination allowed them to be operated by only one through American-style hydraulic tappets. It was unusual and a success for a small European engine. The XR2 was energetic rather than truly swift, costing £5713 in UK, however, it suffered a somewhat choppy ride due to its thick anti roll bar.

There were some good quality conversions in the aftermarket, such as the British Turbo Technics one that increased engine power to 125bhp ((93kW) of which Ford approved at fitting centres without affecting warranty claims. It even sold in Japan through Mazda dealers as Autorama.

Continuously Variable Transmission (CVT) had been introduced on the engaging but ultimately unsuccessful Dutch Daf air-cooled flat-twin of 1959. It was fully automatic, with a centrifugal clutch, limited-slip differential and V-belts running in moveable pulleys. Simple and efficient, the only issue was whether it was worthwhile through being cheap, or because it banished gear changing. Its most practical advantage was negligible power losses, unlike those of conventional automatics with oil-churning torque converters. CVT seemed small-car-friendly and the solitary control for the driver was a forward and reverse lever.

It took 20 years' development of V-belts, manufacturing them in steel segments instead of rubber and textiles, together with

a redesign that pushed (instead of pulling) the belts between the pulleys before CVT was fit for anything as powerful as a Fiesta. Ford preferred to call it Constant Velocity Transmission (CTX) for the 1987 Fiesta II. The engine still whirred a lot as it got up to speed, running ahead, it seemed, of the gearbox. However, it was economical, and with electronic controls the constant buzziness was curbed a little. CVX was optional on the Fiesta and, since it was a joint development between Ford and Fiat from the Daf patents, it appeared on the Fiat Uno also. In the event, customers did not seem ready for it. They continued to prefer the clutches and manual gearboxes to which they were accustomed. *Ford*

Fiesta II: weight 750kg (1653.5lb), 1.1 755kg (1664.5lb). 4-cylinders; transverse; 73.96mm x 55.7mm, 957cc; compr 8.5:1; 33kW (44.25bhp) @ 5750rpm; 34.5kW (46.2bhp)/l; 68Nm (50lbft) @ 3700rpm. 1.1: 73.96 x 64.98mm; 1117cc; 9.5:1; 37kW (49.6bhp) @ 5000rpm; 33.1kW (44.4bhp)/l; 83Nm (61lbft) @ 2700rpm; inverse Ford-Motorcraft carburettor; 3-bearing crankshaft. 1.1: VV carburettor; front wheel drive; sdp clutch; 4-speed synchro; final drive 4.06:1, or 4.29 or 3.84. 1.1: 3.583:1 or 3.842:1. Optional 5-speed. Maximum speed 137kph (85.4mph); 25.9kph (16.1mph) @ 1000rpm (4.06:1); 0-100kph (62mph) 19.8sec; 22.7kg/kW (16.9kg/bhp), 1.1 20.4kg/kW (17kg/bhp); fuel consumption 6.43l/100km (43.9mpg). Price L £4320, 1.1 Ghia £5100. Production 1,980,100 all Fiesta II. Prices were L £5336, Ghia £5657. 1986 1.4 Ghia £6507

FLEXIBLE FIESTAS

Once the Fiesta formula was established, the B-segment model – reference to what its chassis was known as – Ford looked for ways to create alternatives. This was the Fiesta B-platform – the floor plan, engine, transmission, suspension, all the expensive multi-component bits on which to mount different bodies. Sporty cars, luxury cars, vans, and pick-ups could easily be created to increase volumes, essential to keeping down unit costs. The top hampers were the cheap bits. The rest was up to the marketing department.

Concept cars were good for keeping designers on their toes. Motor show specials encouraged ideas, with one of those based on the B-segment podium being the 1985 Ghia Urby. Ford Dearborn was always trying to downsize American cars; it knew that sooner or later gas-guzzlers had to go and the Urby was its way of showing good things could come in small packages. Ford had long established the Ghia design studio in Turin and now its job was to show how roomy a short car could be. Alec Issigonis's radical Mini had shown it was possible – it wasn't commercial as Ford accountants had discovered – but Ghia grasped the idea that people took up less space when they sat upright.

It was not a new idea. It was said that when they started to design the Austin A30 at Longbridge in the 1940s, the first thing they did was set up four chairs with four people on the drawing office floor, draw a line round them and measure that. Here was a common-sense basis for a small car.

The Ghia Urby was 30in shorter than most basic small cars and its designers predicted it could be light enough to be driven by a 1.0 litre engine. They decided that if the roof was a bit taller, 56.4in (143.2cm), with an 86in (218.4cm) wheelbase and overall length of 139.3in (346.2cm) it would be suitable for urban markets, manoeuvrable and easy to park. It was also only 61.2in (155.4cm) wide. Americans were not unaccustomed to parking by shuffling cars along in car parks, "acoustic parking" they called it, so the Urby was made with a polycarbonate front bumper - literally a bumper - with integrated cooling slots. Austin A30s had a 79.5in (201.9cm) wheelbase, were 136.5in (346.7cm) long, 55in (139.7cm) wide and 58.3in (148cm) tall.

Vice-president Design Donald F Kopka was delighted. "The Urby design theme demonstrates that a contemporary aerodynamic appearance can be achieved with a high-seating approach. Its side-view silhouette features a greenhouse that is

Ghia Urby press showing.

relatively far forward. An on-going trend in automotive design."

While the 1985 Ghia Urby occupants sat upright under a raised roof, the 1998 Libre concept at the Chicago Auto Show went further. The Libre exhibited at the Windy City removed the ceiling entirely for what Ford called, "… a fun-to-drive, four-passenger quad-door concept sporty convertible for the entire family." J Mays, V-P Design: "Most small convertibles seat two comfortably. The Libre provides fun for four while retaining the appearance of a two-seat sports car."

Built on the same versatile B-platform as the Fiesta, as well as future Puma, Ka and Courier pick-ups, the Urby had the quad-doors introduced on the Mercury MC4 and used in production extended-cab pickups. The Libre windscreen at 66 degrees still provided headroom with a top up, even though it was not installed on the show car. Finished in bright red metallic with aluminium headlamps, taillamps and exhausts, the headlamps were three individual tubes, two with reflector beams, the third with the amber turn signal lamp. The taillamps were geometric and sat high on the decklid. Libre also appeared at the 1999 Canadian Auto Show in Toronto.

Another flexible Fiesta in 1989 challenged the increasing influence of diesels. Even with a larger, more powerful version of Ford's new compression-ignition engines, Fiesta Mark IIIs using them were not swift. Furthermore, their official fuel consumption figures were not as good, either on the newly introduced official urban cycle or at a constant 90kph (56mph). Although, at 120kph (75mph) they still managed 5.6l/100km (50.4mpg) and acceleration with the optional 5-speed gearbox was slightly faster than a 1.1-litre petrol car, they still seemed leisurely.

In 1992 Ford carried out a bold experiment. It equipped the Fiesta with an engine that had seemed consigned, through inability to meet progressively demanding emission regulations, to the technology dustbin in the 1960s. A 3-cylinder, 2-stroke was equipped with a compressed air fuel metering system so

English perpendicular architecture. Austin designers sat the occupants upright in the A30 launched at the 1951 Motor Show as a "new Austin Seven".

Fiesta lookalike concept Ghia Urby 1985.

precise that its emissions were relatively clean. Unburnt hydrocarbons no longer escaped in such profusion. With the virtue of fewer moving parts, the engine was 100mm (3.9in) lower and 70mm (2.8in) narrower than a 4-cylinder 4-stroke. It had no valves, springs, camshaft, or pushrods, weighed 30 per cent less, showed 12 per cent better economy and 10 per cent more power.

It persuaded Ford to set up a programme running 50 Fiesta 1200cc 2-strokes in field trials. They were astonishingly smooth-running with none of the popping and banging associated with older 2-strokes. They still need lubrication by adding oil to the petrol mixture, a tank under the bonnet supplying enough for 12,500 miles without refilling. Alas, it was another brave initiative that turned out to be problematical and it was concluded.

The 2-stroke 1.2-litre had three cylinders, produced 59.7kW (80bhp) @ 5500rpm; 49.75kW (66.7bhp)/l; 122Nm (90lbft) torque @ 4000rpm. It had reed valve intakes, Sarich forced-air 6bar (87.02psi) fuel injection system by reciprocating pump driven off crankshaft; sealed crankcase; roller-bearing forged one-piece crankshaft and catalytic converter. Top speed was 168kph (104.7mph); it did 0-100kph (62mph) in 10.7sec and 5.7l/100km (49.6mpg).

Concept Fords were made with a purpose. In 1981 Probe III aimed to prepare people for the appearance of Sierra the following year. The Cortina was near the end of its 20 year run, the Probe appearing to be sleeker, aerodynamic, aiming at buyers growing accustomed to coefficients of wind resistance (Cd), hitherto a symptom of speed but now demands for fuel economy were outpacing lust for pace. Fuel crises and ecological demands had educated the clientele. They were sophisticated enough to know "streamlining" was now about more than the pace of sports cars.

The Probe III's job was to get the market ready, and it was drenched in futurist technology, some more wish list than realist because the top floor at Dearborn could

see Sierra was radical and was uncertain if customers would like it. A complex of features, flush windows, the shape of corner pillars, elimination of roof gutters and drip channels, flush wheel discs, rear spats, and plastic skirts, wings and spoilers were combined to give a Cd of 0.22. Curved side windows wound down only after the glass had first moved inwards. Underneath, the airflow was managed just as carefully, the exhaust entirely enclosed within the under-tray and elaborate arrangements were made for insulating heat and noise. Under-car management involved an air scoop that would be retracted on rough roads or to clear town-road obstructions. It was an air-scoop too far as it turned out and never a practicality.

The aerodynamics were so good it was claimed a 1600cc engine, suitably geared, would drive it at 190kph (about 120mph). More importantly, it would provide spectacular economy at any speed. Equipped with car-of-the-future features, digital instruments and what Ford called an Auto Leading and Information (ALI) system, the Probe III gave the driver route guidance. Destinations were programmed, arrows appeared on an animated diagram, but both Dearborn and Dagenham were reading Arthur C Clarke; satellite navigation was in their collective mind long before its time. Sputnik had only been up 23 years since October 1957, and this was looking into the distance. The Probe III was not a runner. It only had one door that opened with later concept Probes, the IV and V, even further removed from any production capability.

The task of the Saetta concept car at the Geneva Motor Show in 1994 was to preview something still smaller, the sub-B class. The small Ford Ka planned for two years hence. If in the event Probe III failed, the prototype Saetta was more of a success. The Saetta was mounted on a shortened Fiesta base following the decision to go ahead with the Sub-B class Ka. The Geneva car was 335cm (131.9in) long and designed by Ford Europe under Claude Lobo. There

Open door, open roof.

was speculation it might get the ingenious two-stroke engine that had undergone field trials in 50 Fiestas of 1989, but there was scant chance. Concept Ka had been around 755kg (1664.5lb), or 75kg (165.3lb) lighter than a Fiesta (the production car was heavier) and according to Richard Parry-Jones, head of product development, the production Ka would have strut front suspension, and he confirmed a Peugeot-style torsion beam rear axle was likely.

Ghia produced another Saetta roadster version of the Ka due to appear at Paris in the autumn. The front was pure Ka, the rear modified and retro-like, in the vogue of the VW concept Beetle and the Renault Fiftie, with a spinal bar following the line of the Ka probably providing structural integrity in the absence of a roof. Resplendent in blue and silver, the Saetta was inspirational, closely following the lines of the approaching production model. The interior was pure Ka, except for patent leather upholstery and silver console mouldings that were a pastiche of 1960s trendiness. Ghia added a tachometer to lend a sporty air, but the Saetta was always more of a fun roadster than a sports car.

Its real significance lay in the introduction of what Ford called New Edge styling, which was to play an important role in shaping Fords of the 1990s and into the 21st century. Camillo Pardo, the American who led the Saetta project at Ghia, said: "It is still edge design, but we are exploring surface development, using softer silhouettes and creases to get away from elliptical shapes."

The Saetta continued to create enormous interest at the Turin Motor Show that autumn. It represented a significant shift in automotive style, confirming that Ford's hangover from the less-than-chic Sierra and Escort era was

Fiesta flights of fancy. Libre Concept shown Chicago.

Pioneer 3-cylinder. Twenty years ahead of an award-winning triple, an experimental 2-stroke was tried out on high-mileage police cars.

Smoothie Sierra. Worried that a radical Cortina replacement would not go down well, Probe III probed opinion.

Geneva Motor Shows were the world motor industry shop window. Saetta was forward planning by concept car.

finally over. It was proof that modish style would be as important in future as technical prowess had been in the past. Ford chiefs remained carefully cautious. Apart from its obvious relationship to the Ka, as soon as the show was over, and Autocar had driven it cautiously on a special preview, it was crated up and flown to Detroit. Senior management on the top floor at Dearborn were now obliged to take it seriously.

The third generation Fiesta, code-named BE13, was launched in January. It looked much the same, the mechanicals were similar, it was still front wheel drive, crosswise engine, but the bodyshell was now 10.2cm (4in) longer and 5.1cm (2in) wider. Wheelbase increased by 15.2cm (6in) providing, for the first time, the option of three-doors or five increasing its family car credentials. This was a process that continued Fiesta to Fiesta year after year. Trendy SUV tastes always encouraged expansion. Fiesta III's basic main lines were 1001cc/1119cc with more space inside, welcome for family Fiestas, as was the 45 per cent bigger boot and 10 per cent more glass. The five-door transformation was not applied to sporty XRs, which seemed to assume hot-hatch buyers preferred lighter, stiffer big-doored coupe styles.

The 18-model range revived old Ford names for marketing, starting with Popular 1.0 3-door £.5199, 5-door £5476; Popular Plus 3-door £5877; Pop Plus 1.1 3-door £6183, 5-door £6460; 1.1L 3-door £6645, 5-door £6922 and LX £7570. Its weight went up; 3-doors 779kg (1717.4lb), 5-doors 785kg (1730.6lb).

Torsion beam rear suspension replaced the old dead rear axle and the front MacPherson struts were modified with the lower arms relocated on double bonded vertical bushes. Making the Fiesta's rear suspension half independent followed a good idea by Volkswagen. The arm on which each wheel swung was joined to its twin by a crosswise steel beam, making the suspension reassuringly strong and keeping the wheels pointing where they should. It worked well. The beam was stout, although owners were advised against jacking the car on it, attaching tow ropes or tie-down chains on ferries or car transporters.

Engine changes met European emission control regulations that would eventually demand the catalytic converters Ford's commendable lean-burn engines had failed to fend off. High Compression Swirl (HCS) combustion chambers with new shapes, port profiles and manifolds, contributed to the debate on the merits of lean burn against exhaust scrubbing as the best means of reducing noxious fumes.

Low-geared steering and unresponsive handling had made the Fiesta still feel rather commonplace, yet that proved to be among its virtues. It had been a best seller for 10 of its 12 years. Production reached 5million, 1.2million of which were sold in Britain where it was soon to push the Sierra off the Dagenham production line. Buyers were obviously fond of it. Valencia and Saarlouis were also working to capacity. Overall cost of ownership was taken seriously by Ford, which claimed average service costs were 27 per cent lower than before. The Fiesta III was better equipped to meet competition from far-east

Ghia's detailing on the Saetta extended to the tail lights.

imports. It now had a radio-cassette player with four speakers, tinted glass, sunroof and metallic paint, all included in the price.

The other big change for the Fiesta III were changes to all the Valencia iron pushrod engines. New cranks and pistons produced different bore/stroke ratios. The former 957cc engine was over-squared at 74x55.7mm, becoming 68.7x67.5mm, making it 1001cc. Power was unchanged, but it was produced at 700 fewer revolutions per minute. The High Compression Swirl (HCS) pushrod engines had fully transistorised ignition using a single flywheel

sensor and a pair of dual output coils instead of the old coil and distributor. The 1.1-litre was given a longer-stroke crank to increase the swept volume; it now had a 75.5mm throw, making it 1119cc, improving economy, raising a few bhp extra and giving more torque. Of the Compound Valve Hemispherical (CVH) overhead cam engines, the 1.4-litre, gained in power and was the first Ford engine to meet European Emission Standards due in 1996. The 1.6-litre was a detuned version of the former carburettor XR2 with 67.1kW (90bhp) instead of 70.8kW (95bhp).

An additional 1.6-litre was the 16-valve Zetec twin cam, as used in the Escort and Mondeo, giving reasonably lively 0-60mph times a fraction over 10sec. The Fiestas' variable ratio rack and pinion steering was not unduly heavy, but the optional power assistance reduced turns lock to lock from the manual's 4.6 to 2.8, enhancing feel and control. In 1991 Valencia donated its three millionth Fiesta to the Queen Sofia fund.

The new Zetec engine had been a long time coming but it was well worth the wait. Japanese motorcycle manufacturer Yamaha, expert in small high-revving multi-cylinder

Fiesta RS Turbo, fastest Fiesta III and, "more fun than a Ferrari" according to The Sunday Times.

Popular Plus brought Fiestas down to earth.

Ghia versions, bigger Fiestas with four doors brought luxury to third generation.

See-through shows beam axle rear, gold disc brakes.

lightweight aluminium engines, was involved in designing and building 1991 prototype Zetec-SEs. Ford's first mass-market 16-valve 1.8-litre was planned for February 1992, beginning with a 1.6-litre for all three small and medium-sized Fords, the Fiesta, Escort, and Orion. It also went into Ford's derivative vans. A more powerful 1.8-litre was phased in over several months and a 2.0-litre Zetec was planned for the Mondeo - still fully a year away. The double overhead cam RS2000 Escort remained, and the existing CVH 1.1-litre and 1.4-litre were planned to go on for a further three years.

The Zetec was produced in Cologne and Mexico, as well as Bridgend in the UK, making a total capacity of a million a year. Developed jointly by Ford's British Dunton and Cologne engineers, the design was thoroughly up to date without being too radical. There was no variable valve timing, as introduced by Honda, or far-reaching structural innovations like Rover's bolted-sandwich K-series. The Zetec's lightweight valve gear with low-mass anti-syphon hydraulic tappets revved smoothly up to 7000rpm before hitting the rev limiter. Its cylinder dimensions were "under-square" and although its block was cast iron in the interests of noise absorption, the 1.8 was still a relative lightweight.

Cam belt replacement was specified at 90,000km (56,000miles), much the same as most of the opposition. After 150,000 hours of dynamometer testing 1260 prototype engines were made, of which 320 were installed in vehicles that covered more than 10million test kilometres (6million miles). In its first form the Zeta was available in two power variants, and subsequently in a variety of sizes. It followed Ford's well-established manufacturing economies in a tradition going back to the 1930s, that allowed the key process of machining the cylinder bores to be done on the same tools their predecessors used. The cylinder centres were exactly the same as those of the CVH it replaced.

Zeta: 1798cc engine, October 1991. Weight 122kg (269lb) with oil and principal fixtures; 4-cyls, in-line; front; transverse; 80.6mm x 88mm, 1798cc; compr 10:1; 77kW (103.3bhp) @ 5500rpm, 42.8kW (57.4bhp)/l; or 96kW (128.7bhp) @ 6250rpm, 53kW (71.6bhp)/l; 153Nm (113lbft) @ 4000rpm or 162Nm (120lbft) @ 4500rpm. Structure: 2 HSN (highly saturated nitrile) toothed belt-driven ohcs; 4-valves, inlet 32mm (1.26in), exhaust 28mm (1.1in); low-mass anti-syphon hydraulic tappets; cylinder head die-cast aluminium, sand-cast grey iron block; chilled cast iron camshafts; high-silicon aluminium pistons; forged steel connecting rods; shell-moulded cast-iron crank with 5 main bearings and 8 counterweights; structural aluminium oil pan; sequential multi-point fuel injection; 16-bit EEC IV engine management computer with 56kB memory; 3-way catalytic converter; fuel requirement 95RON unleaded

Fast Fiestas began with the XR2 in 1981-1983, continuing with the restyling in 1984-1989 and gaining the 1.6 CVH engine. It was only omitted from the model line-up at the beginning of 1989 owing to the priority given mainstream Popular and LX. The 1989-1992 XR2i had the Mark III body still with two doors, 5-speed gearbox, body-coloured bumpers and flared wheel arches to accommodate wider wheels and fatter tyres. It handled well and safely, and with a top speed comfortably over 168kph (105mph) became a firm favourite with keen drivers. Now with fuel injection, necessary in any case for catalytic converter cars, it had a real turn of speed. The suspension was tightened down making it firmer and sportier than its predecessors and, although it never gained the glamour of a VW Golf GTi, it was nevertheless a worthy contender in the hot-hatch market.

The fastest Fiesta was the RS Turbo of 1990. Based on the XR2i, with a 99.2kW (133bhp) CVH engine similar to that in the Escort RS Turbo, it reached 60mph in under eight seconds. Wide wheels and fashionably fat low-profile tyres made the steering heavy at parking speed and it had only a brief production run, being overtaken by the 16-valve RS1800 in 1992.

According to The Sunday Times the RS Turbo was "More fun than a Ferrari at 10 per cent of the price." Sports cars were usually resilient to oil embargoes, but this one had gone on so long it was changing social attitudes. Drivers did not want to look profligate. Entrepreneur owners of Ferraris sometimes preferred to leave them in the garage and get their kicks discreetly in a Fiesta RS with wide wheel arches and roof spoiler. It was not entirely decorous; it was more circumspect than an XR2i with gaudy blue piping, yet it was not so obvious as a gas-guzzling 12-cylinder.

The RS could, however, suffer from a familiar problem with powerful front wheel

Zetec aluminium engines were a revelation. This was to be the way ahead for Fiesta and its successor. Sixteen valves for the Fiesta, Escort, and Orion.

drive cars. It could be unruly in the wet, with kart-like sensitivity that demanded constant attention if it was not to dash disconcertingly from kerb to kerb. This was a severe price of directness that might have been helped by power-assisted steering but to keep the price under target, that was not included. Experienced racing and rally drivers could cope with the problem quite easily, but as insurance assessors discovered, it could catch out the unwary.

The engagingly light and sensitive steering was heavy in town. Fat, fashionable, low-profile tyres which gave the front wheels good grip at speed meant heaving the wheel round at parking speeds and the firm ride was turbulent on rough roads. Occupants bobbing about was perhaps a small price to pay for good handling. Belted securely into the supportive Recaro racing-style seats could be like riding a roller-coaster, but the sense of command was commendable, although it

XR2i: Alloy wheels became standard by summer 1990.

RS1800 and RS Turbo were the fastest Fiestas yet in a highly contested "hot-hatch" market.

did not stick, leech-like, to corners. It would slide outwards, like a well-balanced sports car giving a driver plenty of warning when it is about run wide. It was controllable, fast and nimble.

The Fiesta RS was not notably economical. It reached 60mph in well under 8 seconds leaving every other Ford, save the Cosworth, trailing. It did 207kph (130mph) and being small and light meant it could dart swiftly through traffic almost as nimbly as a motorcycle. On point-to-point journeys it would probably keep up with most Ferraris, but doing so might use almost as much fuel, swirling into the small and exquisitely engineered 133 horsepower 1.6 litre engine at a rate of only 12.3-11.3l/100km (23-25mpg). This worsened if its startling acceleration was much used. The answer was to drive as slowly as an ordinary XR2i, when it might ascend to 33-35mpg. On the road the RS cost £9995.

There was more to come. Peugeot's 205 GTi was dominating speedy small cars, and even after becoming the XR2i, the Fiesta was no match. At around 190kph (118mph) it was fast, but lacked the Peugeot's precision, quick steering, and exquisite balance and even the April 1990 RS Turbo at the Turin Motor Show, still fell short. Although, 1.6sec faster than the XR2i to 100kph (62mph), it

was slower than the lighter Renault 5 GT Turbo. The Fiesta's CVH engine had been based on the Escort's with a Garrett T02 turbocharger and air-to-air intercooler.

The short-lived Turbo model was replaced in 1992. The RS1800 resurrected the name of an Escort rather than a Fiesta and although slower, with a 16-valve version of an engine still called Zeta rather than Zetec, overall it was an improvement. The ride was still choppy, a result of the addition of a rear anti-roll bar, but the smooth-running engine was a revelation after the uncouth turbo. It had ample torque and was agreeably economical. The RS Fiesta had Recaro seats, 5-spoke alloy wheels, and the obligatory cosmetic bounce was provided by a colour-keyed spoiler, even though the steering had reverted to over four turns lock to lock.

Fiesta RS: 1800 RS Turbo items labelled RST. Body saloon; 3-doors, 5-seats; weight 995kg (2193.6lb), RST 920kg (2028lb). Engine 4-cylinders, front, transverse; 80.6mm x 88mm, 1796cc; compr 10:1; 96kW (128.7bhp) @ 6250rpm; 54.6kW (71.7bhp)/l; 162Nm (120lbft) @ 4500rpm. RST 80 x 79.5mm; 1598cc; compr 8.2:1; 98kW (131.4bhp) @ 5500rpm; 61.3kW (82.2bhp)/l; 184Nm (136lbft) @ 2400rpm.

Zeta, 2 belt-driven overhead camshafts; hydraulic tappets; 4-valves; aluminium cylinder head, iron block; electronic fuel injection, breakerless electronic ignition; 5-bearing crankshaft. RST CVH 1 ohc; 2-valves; Bosch K-Jetronic injection; GarrettT02 turbocharger, intercooler. Front wheel drive; sdp diaphragm spring clutch, 5-speed synchromesh; final drive 3.82:1. Steel monocoque; ifs by MacPherson struts; irs by trailing arms, torsion beams, coil springs; telescopic dampers; anti-roll bars front and back; hydraulic brakes, front 24cm (9.5in) ventilated discs, rear 18cm (7.5in) drums; rack and pinion steering; 42l (9.2gal) tank; 185/55VR14 tyres 5.5J rims. Wheelbase 244.5cm (96.3in); track front 140.5cm (55.3in), rear 137.5cm (54.1in); length 380cm (149.6in); width 163cm (64.2in); height 132.5cm (52.2in); ground clearance 14cm (5.5in); turning circle 9.8m (32.2ft). Equipment: radio/cassette, 4-speakers, tinted glass, sunroof, metallic paint all standard. Maximum speed 200kph (124.6mph), RST 205kph (127.7mph); 30kph (18.7mph) @ 1000rpm, RST 33.8kph (21.1mph) @ 1000rpm; 0-100kph (62mph) 8.5sec, RST 8.2sec; 10.4kg/kW (7.7kg/bhp), RST 9.4kg/kW (7kg/bhp); fuel consumption 8l/100km (35.3mpg). Price RS Turbo 1991 £11,731, RS1800 1992 £11,615.

FIESTA SPINOFF:
PUMA ONE

Once the Fiesta's RS and XR versions were no more, new ways had to be found of extending the reach of a prescription that had been so successful. None of the Fiesta offshoots did more to enhance the image than the Puma. Right from the start Richard Parry-Jones, Vice-President Small-Medium Vehicle Centre set the tone, "The Puma represents Ford's focus on the special needs of the enthusiast driver. It's a car developed specifically for a rewarding driving experience. The Puma is a visible symbol of all the driver-oriented strengths that we're now consistently building into our cars."

Its bullet points, according to Ford were: A distinctive new sports coupé for rewarding driving; 1.7-litre Zetec SE engine, with fully variable cam timing; Agile chassis tuned for steering and handling; Power steering and anti-lock brakes; Sleek, classic styling with fresh design cues; Affordable, with a low cost-of-ownership; Comprehensive safety and security packages and individual seats for four adults, plus generous boot.

"Ford's compact new sports coupé, the Puma, combines distinctive and dynamic styling with a new, high-performance 1.7-litre engine and an agile chassis developed to give a rewarding driving experience. It represents an exciting opportunity for Ford and is the company's first entry into the small sports coupé market," according to Chairman and Managing Director Ian McAllister. "It is designed to meet the needs of a growing number of performance enthusiasts who are demanding a distinctive looking coupé

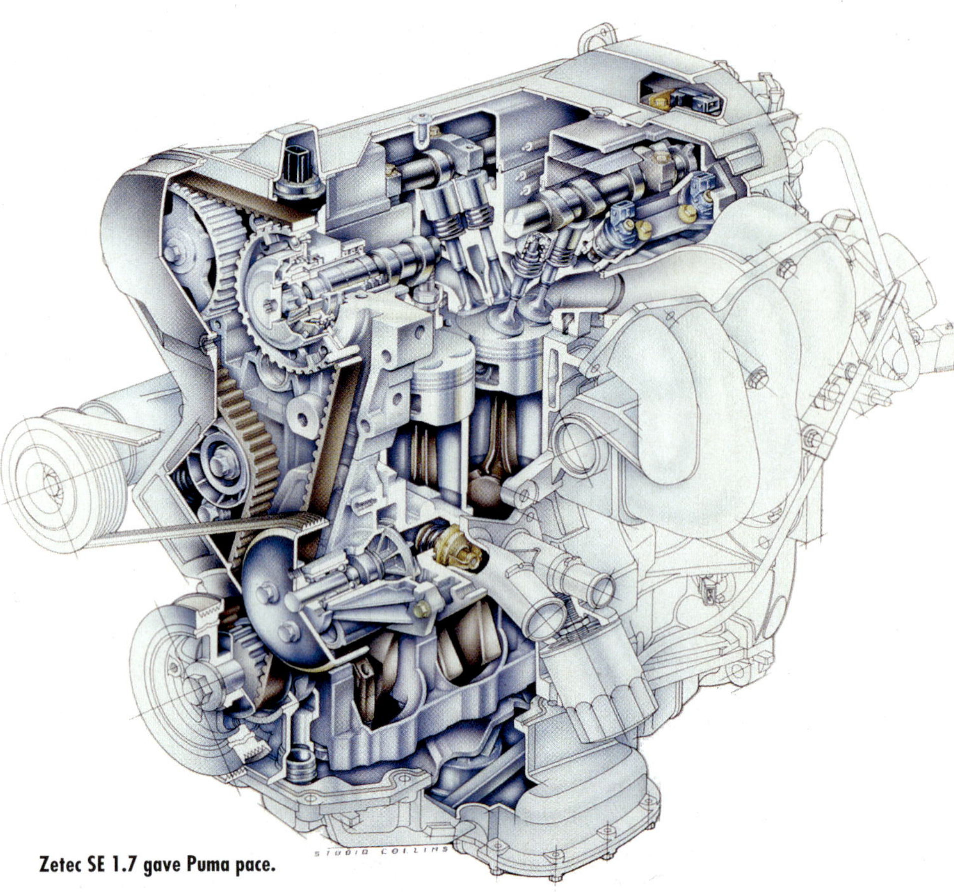

Zetec SE 1.7 gave Puma pace.

which also provides a high level of driving dynamics and functionality. The Puma was created to provide a wellrounded package at an affordable price. Ownership costs are moderate, too, with good fuel economy and best-in-class servicing costs. With its launch, Ford now has the broadest passenger car range in the UK – from the innovative Ka to the recently launched Explorer".

It was extravagant praise but thoroughly deserved. The 3-door Puma was a single model, with one trim level and an up-to-date safety and security package.

It was still vital to get the most out of each platform and code-named SE161 was based, like the Ka, on the much-improved Fiesta introduced at the same Geneva Motor Show. The Lynx concept at the 1996 Geneva, like the Saetta, had curved roof hoops of carbon fibre but extended, rather than foreshortened the Fiesta framework by 25cm (9.8in) to 408cm (160.6in), some 4cm (1.6in) longer than an Escort.

Production Pumas retained the Fiesta wheelbase and carried on Ka-type New Edge styling, rounded off to the talented Ian Callum's design in tune with the sporty theme. Instead of the Ka's modest pushrods, its Yamaha-inspired 16-valve Zetec-SE with Variable Camshaft Timing (VCT), shifted the inlet valves' phasing, though not their lift or dwell, according to engine speed and load. VCT's unique feature was continuous electronic operation rather than being prompted by anything mechanical. The Puma also gained a forged steel crankshaft. "A crankshaft that's bending is a crankshaft you can hear," according to Richard Parry-Jones. Twenty per cent of the Puma was different from the Fiesta, mostly important expensive bits.

Callum, who shaped the Puma, was an automotive Gucci, Ghia or Giugiaro from Dumfries. Cars were fashion icons and some

of the best came from Ian and his brother Moray Callum, suggesting there may have been more to Dumfries than Robert Burns, JM Barrie, David Coulthard, and John Paul Jones. The brothers were joint recipients of the 2006 Jim Clark Memorial Trophy, awarded to Scots who made a major contribution to the world of motoring. Ian became Director of Design at Jaguar, and Moray his opposite number at Mazda, until being appointed Design Director of Ford Cars for the Americas.

Ian Callum was single-minded about car design and in particular about Jaguar. Aged 13 in 1968, he wrote to WM Heynes, Jaguar's vice chairman (engineering) and technical director, enclosing sketches and enquiring earnestly how he should go about joining the industry. Company culture at Jaguar treated such approaches with the gravity they deserved. Bill Heynes was instrumental in Jaguar engineering from 1935, and with William (later Sir William) Lyons, Walter Hassan, and Len Baily created the legendary XK engine. Yet he took the time to write a formal reply to Master I S Callum, Glencaird, Glencaple Road Dumfries.

"Dear Ian, I thank you for your letter and drawings, which I have had a good look at. Your general conception and ideas are good… engineering drawing training is necessary… you should take this up at school in such a way that it does not interfere with your other studies. It is apparent that you intend to enter the styling side of the industry… you would do well to take some art training in due course as you have obviously a flair for this side of the business…"

Eleven years later Ian Callum joined Ford, working on the Fiesta, the Ford RS200 mid-engined rally car, the Escort RS Cosworth, the Mondeo and the Puma. Joining Tom Walkinshaw Racing, he designed the

Reflections on crisply
shaped Pumas.

exquisite Aston Martin DB7, for which he had already won a Jim Clark Award. With Ford's Premier Automotive Group, he worked on the Range Rover, before realizing his ambition to go to Jaguar where he was responsible for the aluminium Jaguar XK. "It looks just like a Jaguar should – powerful and exciting. That comes from a sense of tension, muscle and form and is very much part of the design language we create."

The Ford Puma was his mini masterpiece. Its body shell was stiffer than the Fiesta's, 1mm extra on the front anti-roll bar, five per cent up on spring rates, and 30 per cent on the rear suspension's twist beam made

it far more of a driving enthusiast's car than any regular Fiesta. This was a coupe and hot-hatch with stiffer springing, 12mm lower suspension, an extra 20 per cent roll stiffness and different rebound damping at the back. Parry-Jones was convinced Puma owners would prefer sporty characteristics, like sharper turn-in and a short-travel gearshift, rather than a harsh ride and noise level of an out and out sports racer. They would be prepared to put up with high loading sill of the boot, in return for more torsional body strength, so crucial for good handling. The high-tech appearance was sustained by smooth headlight lenses and what was known

as acoustic engineering-set noise targets. Ford called this a "Sound signature" and the close-fitting window frames echoed Callum's Jaguar XK8 window line.

Road testers applauded it, finding Pumas surprisingly quiet and refined, even at speed. Clever details included equipping them with tyres that had an anti-aquaplaning groove in the middle, like those Dunlop technician Iain Mills used to cut by hand for Jackie Stewart's Formula 1 Tyrrell. Motor racing did sometimes affect car technology.

Press comment was concerned about details. It was critical of the thickness of windscreen pillars that obstructed vision quite

Callum masterpiece. Puma looked as though it had the speed of his Aston Martin DB7.

Well-proportioned Puma.

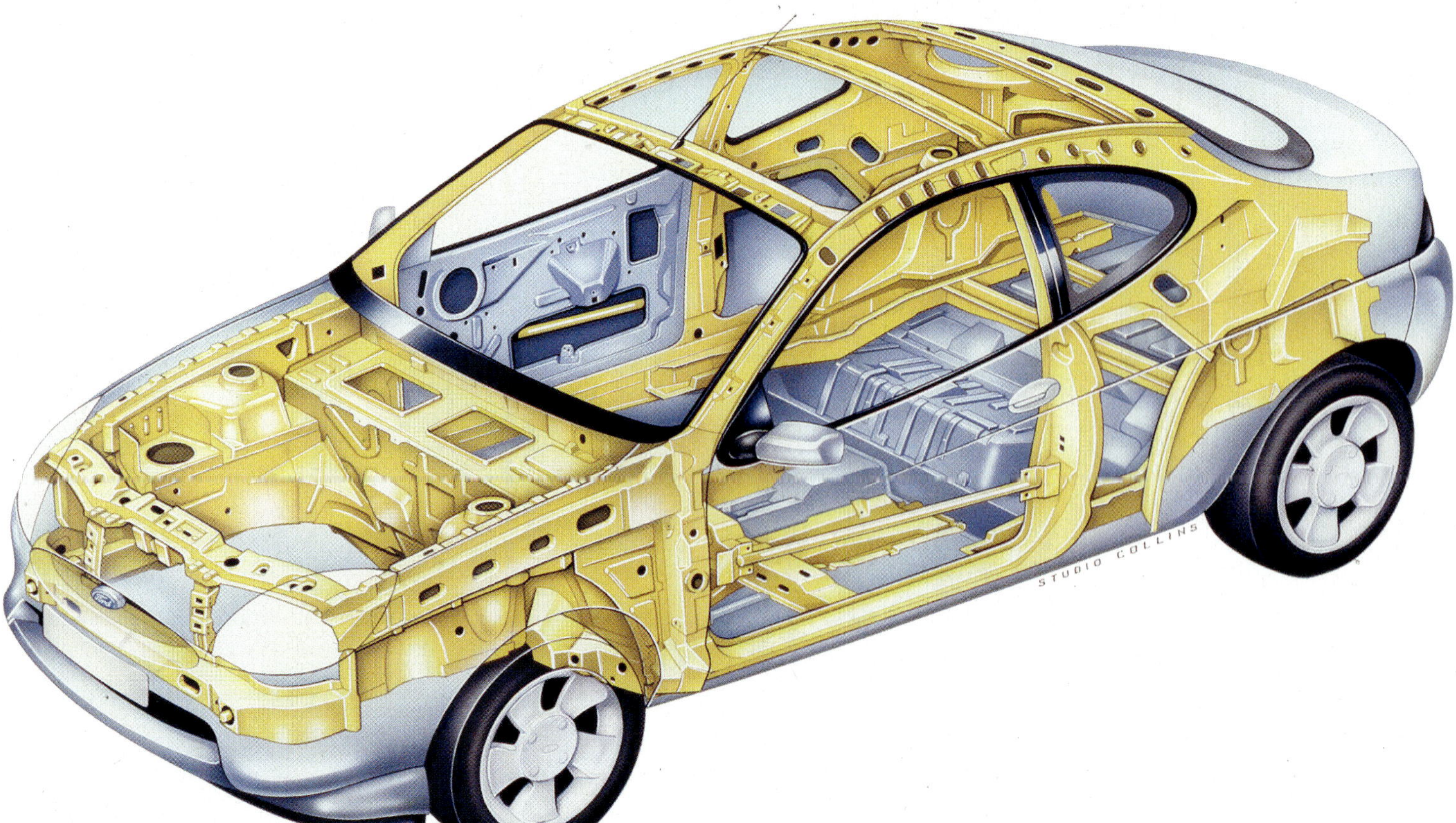

Fiesta floor. Puma bodyshell

Ian (centre) and Moray Callum brothers in design receive ASMW Jim Clark Award from Stephen Park.

a lot, dubious about Parry-Jones's careful orchestration of engine noises, describing it as an "ersatz" philosophy and "not quite the real thing". One wrote "I suppose you're going to have to concede that there's something slightly flaky about it. The mock wood on the inside of the Scorpio, and the mock aluminium in the inside of the Puma, not to mention the engine tuning quite literally like an organ pipe to make it sound right, does tend to give the impression that there's quite a lot about Fords which is contrived."

One area where no imitation was possible was handling and road holding. The Puma came out well as enjoyable, riding more firmly than a Fiesta without any of the coarseness associated with a track-ready sports car. "Having one on a week-long road test confirms most things, especially its reassuring enjoyment element. The seats felt curious to begin with - a very high roll of upholstery under your knees - but this disappears after a day or so and the result is very supportive. It is subtly done. You don't have to brace yourself for fast cornering. It does corner fast. Feels very stable. The good seating makes the handling feel even better. The only shortcoming is fore-and-aft pitching

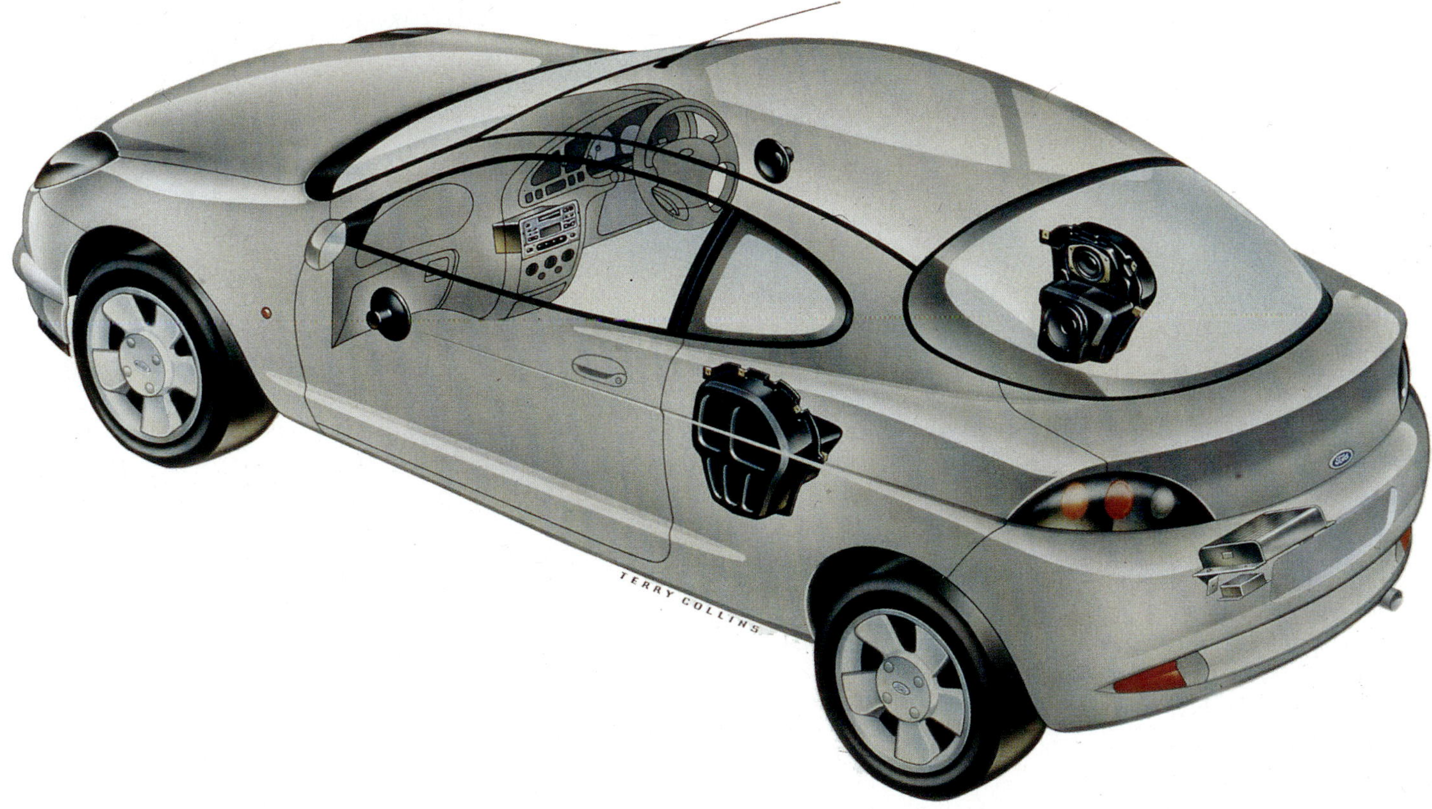

Puma sound system.

Puma. Save the name for later.

as a result of the short Fiesta wheelbase. Richard Parry-Jones was right, the boot's big and you don't mind the high sill. My daughter suggested knitting a woolly hat for the cold metal gear lever knob on cold mornings. I am sure I could live with a Puma; it is pretty, and a bit like a born-again Austin-Healey Sprite for hustling along country roads feeling you are going twice as fast as you really are. It would have to be a very determined Porsche 911 that could outpace you on a twisty road. Yet like a Sprite the steering is sensitive enough to need all your attention."

That writer was as good as his word. He bought a Puma and kept it ten years.

There was applause for the optional equipment – passenger airbag, infra-red central locking, air conditioning and radio. Air conditioning was £350 and a GSM hands-free phone £35. The mini-sports coupe gained a 12E insurance group. A modest 5000 Pumas a year were expected for UK with the intention of relatively limited special editions that would keep residual values high. In the fact, Pumas were so popular up to 35,000 were made in its peak year and 20,000 every year thereafter. Made alongside the Fiesta on the same production line, it went on sale in the first week of July for £14,550 and was promoted in a Steve McQueen TV commercial.

In the summer of 1998, a 1.4-litre Puma was presented as an alternative to the 1.7. It cost some £1500 less, was 28kg (61.7lb) lighter, and took 2seconds longer to reach 100kph (62mph). It was 19.3kph (12mph) slower but had a fuel consumption advantage of some 15 per cent. The Zetec-SE engine from the 1.4 Fiesta was smoother running than the 1.7, the difference in performance quite small and it ran on the same 15in alloy wheels and 195/50 tyres as the 1.7, so the handling was every bit as good. There was less likelihood of wheelspin in the wet, or on loose surfaces, but as a stylish two-plus-two coupe it suffered from the same cramped rear seats and unevenly shaped boot. The 1.4i cost £13,200 and was produced until 2001 with 45,000 being sold in the UK.

In 1999 a 223.7kW (300bhp) concept Puma with stretched wheelbase and four-wheel drive (it was really an Escort Cosworth with longitudinal engine and steroid Puma bodywork) was exhibited at the Geneva Motor Show. Ford Racing Division at Boreham developed a ST160 Puma, based more on the production car, with 119.3kW (160bhp), front wheel drive and limited slip differential. Brakes were bigger, with Alcon racing callipers, it did 225kph (140mph) and in the autumn the go-ahead was given for up to 1000 to be built for racing by Tickford at Daventry, Northamptonshire, priced at £23,000. Another limited edition Racing Puma had 114.1kW (153bhp) and extended aluminium wheel arches, for £22,750. Last of all the £13,995 Puma Thunder came in Magnum Grey, or Moondust with black leather trim. *Ford*

PUMA 1.7: Feb 1997 to November 2001. Coupe; 2-doors, 2+2-seats; weight 1039kg (2290.6lb). 4-cylinders, front; transverse; 80mm x 83.5mm, 1679cc; compr 10.3:1; 92kW (123.4bhp) @ 6300rpm; 54.8kW (73.5bhp)/l; 157Nm (116lbft) @ 4500rpm. Zetec-SE twin belt-driven ohc, 4-valve; variable camshaft timing; aluminium head, and block; Ford EEC-V multipoint fuel injection, electronic ignition; 5-bearing crankshaft. Front wheel drive; 5-speed synchromesh; final drive 3.82:1. Steel monocoque; ifs by MacPherson strut, offset coil springs, lower A-arms, anti-roll bar; rear suspension semi-independent twist beam with coil spring damper units; hydraulic servo brakes, front 24cm (9.5in) disc, rear drums, ABS; rack and pinion variable PAS; 42l (9.2gal) tank; 195/50R15 tyres, 6J rims. Wheelbase 245cm (96.5in); track 145cm (57.1in) front, 141cm (55.5in) rear; length 398.5cm (156.9in); width 167.5cm (65.9in); height 134cm (52.8in); ground clearance 14cm (5.5in); turning circle 10.4m (34.1ft). Alloy wheels, metallic paint £240, passenger airbag £300, air conditioning £350. Maximum 197.5kph (123mph) Autocar; 31.4kph (19.6mph) @ 1000rpm; 0-100kph (62mph) 8.6sec; 11.3kg/kW (8.4kg/bhp); fuel consumption 7.4l/100km (38.2mpg). £14,550. 45,000 UK sales.

AN51 XMY

Ford coined Classic to move up-market.

Oval grille for fourth edition Fiesta.

Millennium Fiesta refreshed with smaller grille in 1999.

FIESTA IV: FIESTA GOES CLASSIC

Old habits died hard. Just as the Populars of 1950s and 1960s were born-again versions of superseded models, in the 1990s Fiestas of the 1980s were similarly resuscitated but Popular sounded a bit too Bargain Basement. A new name had to be coined implying continuity and good value. So, furnished with 1.1, 1.3, and diesel engines, as well as different trim versions they were distinguished as Quartz and Cabaret 3- and 5-door. They were also called Classic. It had a ring. Classic cars made buyers think 'appreciating asset'.

Prices were much the same, with power steering an option for £430 on the front-end-heavy diesels. The 1.3 was a 152.5kph (95mph) car and reached 100kph (62mph) in 14.2sec. The more economical diesel, with much the same power to weight ratio, was only a shade slower at 150.9kph

(94mph) and a languid 15.4sec. Launched originally in 1976 for the lighter-weight front-rank Fiesta, the all-iron pushrod crossflow 2-valve engine, now designated Endura-E was inherited from the 1967 Cortina Mark II. Despite much modification over the years, however, it was past its best and although it had acquired fuel injection necessary for the new stringent emission requirements, it didn't have much power.

Anxious to obtain lower insurance groups for 1994, Ford took a lower-key approach to speed achieving entry into Group 7e for the Fiesta 1.4 Si, compared to 14 with the old XR2's. The 1.6 litre Si sat in Group 8e. The 'e' suffix denoted insurance industry approval for new measures to make Fiestas more secure against car theft.

The Fiesta IV had stronger bodywork for better crash resistance and although the

shape scarcely changed beyond new side mouldings, thicker metal stiffened the engine bay, crossmembers under the floor, and main connections between the door pillars, sills and roof rails. The sheet metal surrounding the door aperture, the door itself and the body floor area were all modified to improve it no matter what direction an accident came from. A brace was added between the floor and the steering column to reduce its movement in a frontal impact. The facia bulkhead was made thicker and acted as a crosscar beam to absorb and distribute side impact energy. There were airbags, new interiors, and power steering.

FIESTA CLASSIC: 74mm x 55.7mm 957cc provided 33.6kW (45bhp) @ 6000rpm, and the 74 x 65mm 1117cc 39.5kW (53bhp) @ 6000rpm. From 1989 Fiesta IIIs 1.3: 74mm x 75.5mm, 1299cc; cr 8.8:1; 44kw (59bhp) @ 5000rpm; 33.9kW (45.4bhp)/l; 103Nm (76lbft) @ 2500rpm and a diesel 82.5 x 82mm; 1753cc; compr 21.5:1; 44kW (59bhp) @ 4800rpm; 25.1kW (33.7bhp)/l; 110Nm (81lbft) @ 2500rpm, which did 5.3l/100km (53.3mpg). Price in 1997 1.1 £7615-£8015; 1.1 Quartz £8015-8445; 1.3 Cabaret £8415-£8845; 1.8D £8040-£8470; 1.8D Quartz £8440-£8870.

The smallest engine was a 1.1 litre, producing 50bhp and modest performance. There was a 60bhp 1.3litre, and the electronic fuel injection on the 1.4litre CVH engine from the previous Fiesta was updated to increase its power from 71 to 75 bhp. Its best pulling speed was reduced from 4,000 to 2,800rpm making it feel more flexible, quickening its pace from 0 to 60 mph from 14.2 to 12.8 seconds.

The 1.4 EFI was the first Ford engine that met the European exhaust emission standards due from 1996. Improved fuel injection increased

Fiesta Finesse for 1998.

power a little and there was also the 90bhp 1.6 litre Zetec 16valve engine, used in the Escort and Mondeo, achieving 0 to 60mph only a shade over the 10 second benchmark. The Si 1.4 litre cost £9,450, the 1.6 litre £9,995. Road testers at the time found lively and smooth running, although neither the 110mph 1.6 litre nor the 104mph 1.4 were thought an adequate replacement for the 116mph XR2, despite it handling like one. Ford claimed it met customer demand for greater convenience, comfort, and equipment levels than the XR2. It was certainly a good deal quieter, and most owners could expect see 36-40mpg. Anti-lock brakes still came at an extra cost.

The effect of new trim fabrics, and the choice of either Pumice or Raven to match exterior body colours on LX and Ghia was scarcely convincing. Fussy materials felt tacky, and appearances were not helped by poor detailing. Seats had large shoulder supports, and there did not seem to be any more space in the car now than there was before. A big hand-wheel operated the glass sunroof and there was no panel to cover up on the inside. It looked cheap and lacked style.

Outside had been more cleverly redone, with a large moulding for the front bumper and air intake, with two built-in lamps, and another large bumper moulding at the back, tidied up the appearance. Power steering was worthwhile. Fiestas already had variable ratio rack-and-pinion steering, light at speed and not unduly heavy for parking, but the new installation had been tightened up to only 2.8 turns from lock to lock against the manual's 4.6, improving both feel and control. PAS was available with all engines except the 1.1 HCS (which was lighter than the CVH and 16V and put less load on the front tyres) and the 1.3 automatic.

Safety was taken to new lengths. Dynamic Safety Engineering (DSE) was a programme applied to Mondeo, to a redesign of the 1993 Escort, the Transit van, as well as Granada and Scorpio. It put a steel cage round a car's occupants to absorb the energy of a crash and reduce the loads on seat belts. The objective was to distribute crash forces through what Ford called stress paths and entailed virtually redesigning the Fiesta's body.

By now all Fiestas had a driver's side airbag in the steering wheel hub, and the option of a front passenger airbag. There was more space in front of the passenger, so while the driver's airbag had a volume of 30 litres, the passenger's was bigger at 60 litres. A high security doublelocking system and Ford's new electronic passive antitheft system, called Safeguard, became standard on all petrol engined Fiestas. A tiny electronic transponder in the ignition key prevented the engine being started, providing a high security lockout system that could only be switched on by the correct signal from 49.3 billion possible codes. This prevented 'hot wiring' the ignition and Ford claimed virtually eliminated risk of unauthorised use or theft. The miniature transponder was like those used for security tags in clothing stores and activated a transceiver around the steering lock. It needed no independent battery power and there were no electrical connections between the elements.

The Fiesta also became available for the first time with doublelocking, linked to a central control operated by either of the front

Fiesta Zetec S2 hard-wearing comfortable interior trim.

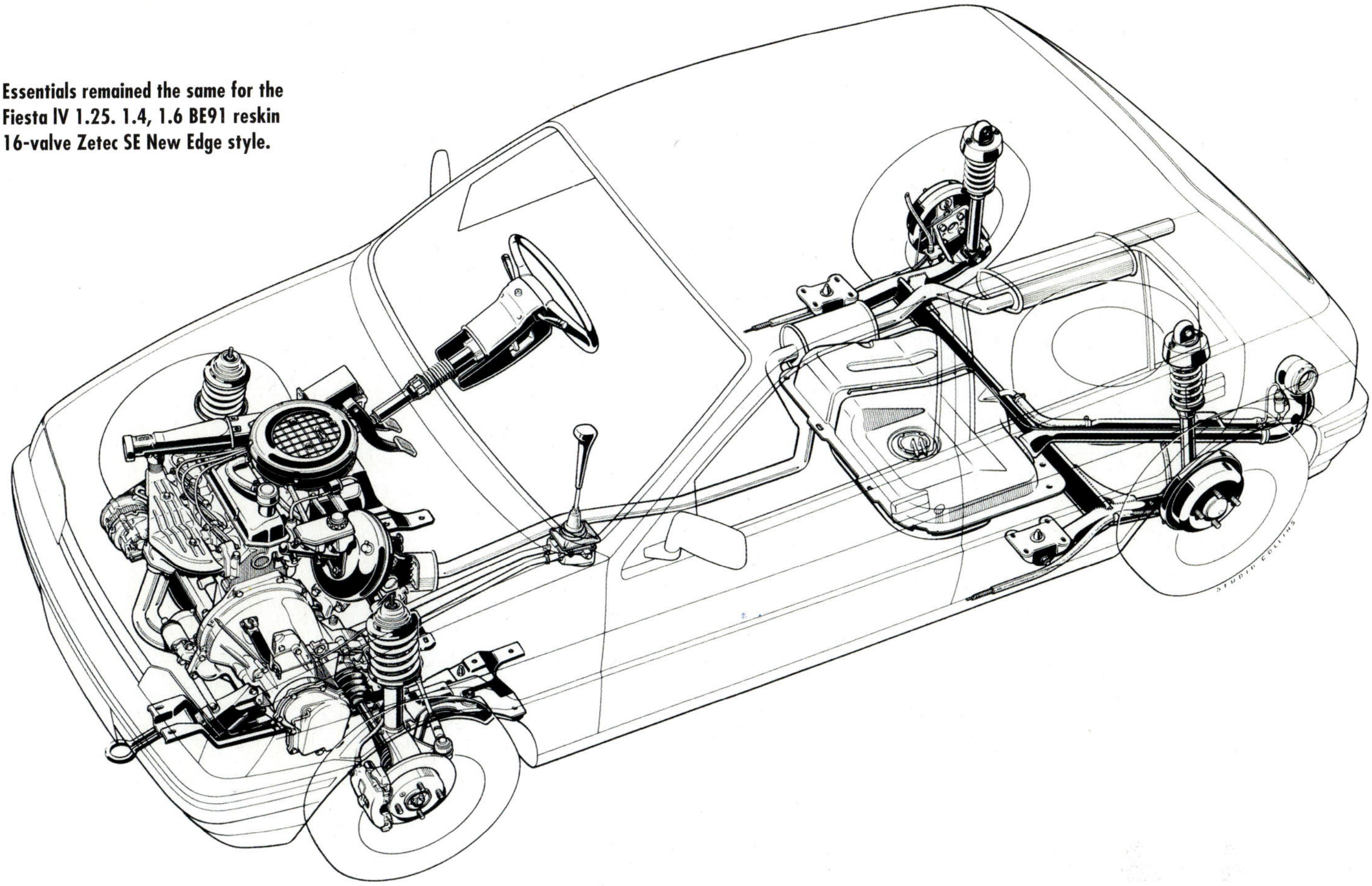

Essentials remained the same for the Fiesta IV 1.25. 1.4, 1.6 BE91 reskin 16-valve Zetec SE New Edge style.

doors. Once the double locks had been set by turning the key in the door, only that would release the locks again and they could not be opened from the inside. All lock mechanisms were shielded by shrouded cables instead of rods, making interference difficult.

BE91 was code for the 1996 complete reskin round the 16-valve Zetec-SE engine and made the Fiesta Mark IV Britain's best-selling car from 1996 to 1998. The platform was much the same, but this time the body was more extensively altered, notably the side door casings. It failed to gain the Ka's bold New Edge, but the corporate oval grille made it look sufficiently different to reassure customers they were buying the newest. Constant changes were still a cornerstone of marketing in the 1990s. The Zetec-SE was smoother and quieter, and the dohc 16-valve engine represented more than merely a redesign of the top end. It was wholly aluminium instead of iron and aluminium, cast-in ribs maintaining the structural stiffness necessary to reduce vibrations. The previous Zetec's hydraulic tappets were discontinued, the new engine reverted to plain mechanical means of operating valves, yet it marked notable progress towards being almost maintenance-free.

By the 1990s cars were expected to need less attention. Oil changes were scheduled for 10,000 miles, new spark plugs at 30,000 miles, and routine valve clearance checks at 100,000 miles. At just 89kg (196.2lb) engines weighed less than half their predecessor's 122kg (269lb), not only because of the

Diesels were doing better, 4-doors 1996.

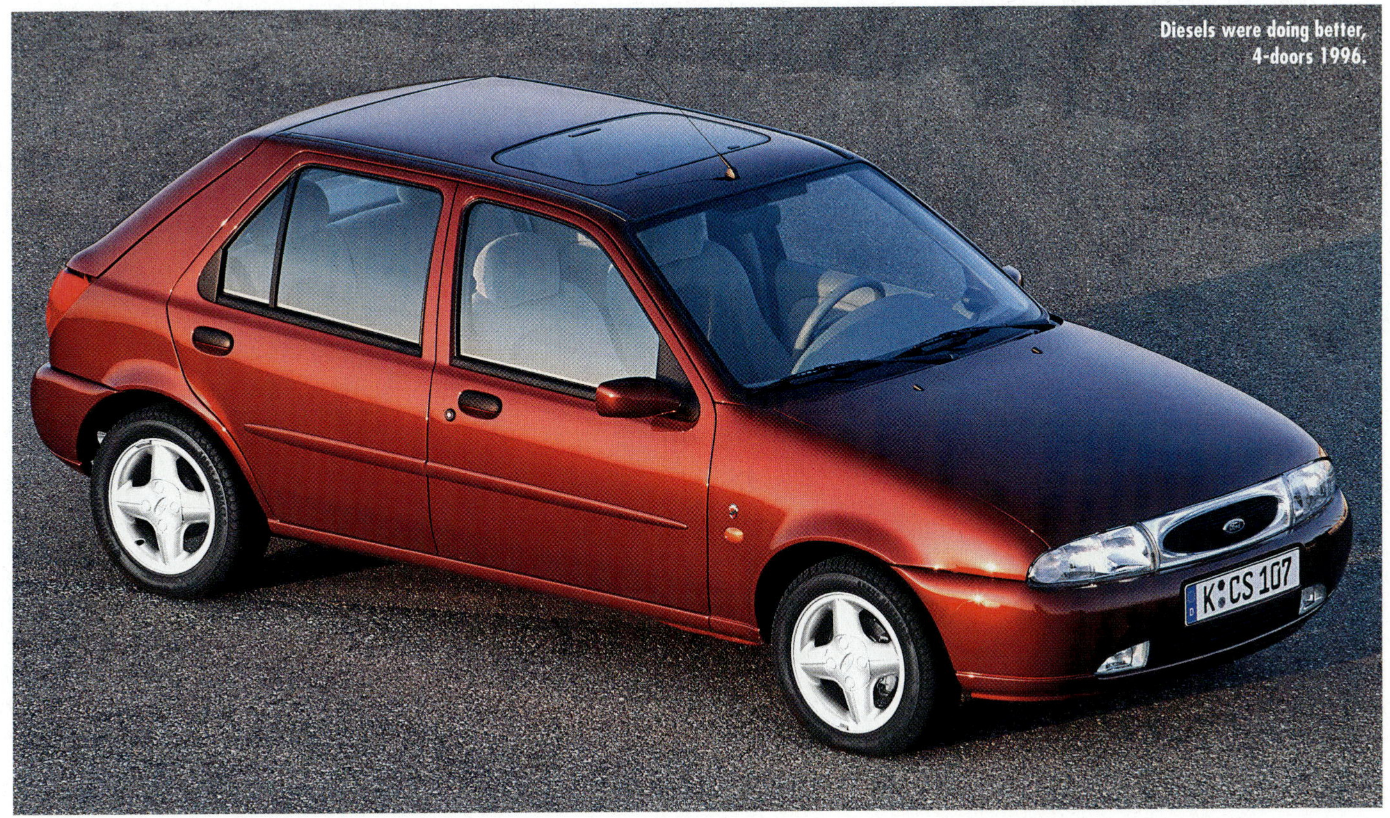

Fiesta came joint top with the Nissan Micra in *What Car?'s* security tests. Burglars were unable to break through the fixed allocation of deadlocks inside two minutes.

A Fiesta festooned with deckchair seats, airbags and big doorpocket.

aluminium, but also from making components such as the complex inlet valve tracts of plastic and cam covers from magnesium alloy. Weight reduction was key to a lively performance, improving fuel consumption, and keeping production costs down.

BE91: January 1996. Saloon; 3/5-doors, 4-seats; weight 940kg (2072.3lb). 4-cylinders, front; transverse; 71.9mm x 76.5mm, 1242cc; compr 10:1; 55kW (73.8bhp) @ 5200rpm; 44.3kW (59.4bhp)/l; 110Nm (81lbft) @ 4000rpm. 1.4: 76 x 76.5mm, 1388cc; 66kW (88.5bhp) @ 5500rpm; 47.6kW (63.8bhp)/l; 122Nm (90lbft) @ 4000rpm. 2 belt-driven ohc; 4-valve; aluminium head and block; EEC-V multi-point sequential fuel injection, distributorless electronic ignition; 5-bearing crankshaft. front wheel drive; 5-speed synchromesh; final drive 4.27:1. 1.4, 3.84:1. Steel monocoque; ifs by MacPherson struts, coil springs, anti-roll bar; rear suspension torsion beam axle; telescopic dampers; hydraulic, vacuum servo 24cm (9.45in) front ventilated disc brakes; rear drums 19.1cm (7.5in); rack and pinion PAS; 42l (9.2 gal); 145R-13, 155/70R-13 or 165R-13 tyres, 4.5 or 5J rims. Wheelbase 244.5cm (96.3in); track 143cm (56.3in) front, 137.5cm (54.1in) rear; length 383cm (150.8in); width 163cm (64.2in); height 141cm (55.5in); ground clearance 14cm (5.5in); turning circle 10.3m (33.8ft). ABS optional; driver's side airbag, Ford stereo, PAS, electric sunroof standard. Maximum speed 170kph (105.9mph), 1.4 171.8kph (107mph); 30.9kph (19.3mph) @ 1000rpm; 0-100kph (62mph) 12.7sec, 1.4 10.7sec; 17.1kg/kW (12.7kg/bhp); fuel con 6l/100km (47.08mpg), 1.4 6.2l/100km (45.6mpg). 1.25 Cfi 3-door Encore £9965, 5-door Si £10335, Ghia £10630. 1.4Si

£10,750, option packs £395 and £225, air conditioning £470. 1.6i Encore CTX £11,700; 1.6i L CTX £12,135.

In January 1996 the Fiesta platform was reinforced to improve refinement and stretched to include a crushable area at the front, now mandatory almost everywhere. The gearbox casing was webbed and ribbed to reduce noise, enhancing the roadworthiness of both the Fiesta and Mondeo. Now the responsibility of Richard Parry-Jones, a skilful engineer accountable for all Ford's European small and medium cars, together with consultant Sir Jackie Stewart, wrought a substantial improvement in the behaviour of the entire range, ironically achieved when Ford's involvement in international motor racing was diminished.

Attention was concentrated on more practical, seemingly mundane matters, such as the flourishing diesel market, neglected because Ford had yet to be convinced it was going to be sustained. The Fiesta diesel was a development of the overhead cam 1.8 litre from the old CVH range, now known as Endura-DE, although it was not yet turbocharged to give it the performance on par with its petrol counterparts. Diesels had never caught on in America and Detroit was always suspicious of them. However, with fuel prices and fiscal policies in Europe, these seemed to secure it meantime although anomalies persisted. Ford's attitude to the development of diesels was not matched by the UK government's curious stance that kept the price of diesel fuel high.

FIESTA DIESEL ENDURA DE: 3/5-doors, 4-seats; weight 1020kg (2248.7lb); 4-cylinders, front; transverse; 82.5mm x 82mm, 1753cc; compr 21.5:1; 44kW (59bhp) @ 4800rpm; 25.1kW (33.7bhp)/l;

105Nm (77lbft) @ 2500rpm. Single gear and toothed belt driven ohc; 2-valve; iron head and block; fuel injection. ABS optional; standard driver's airbag, Ford stereo, electric sunroof. Maximum speed 155kph (96.6mph); 34.3kph (21.4mph) @ 1000rpm; 0-100kph (62mph) 17.4sec; 23.2kg/kW (17.3kg/bhp); fuel consumption 5.8l/100km (48.7mpg). 1.8D Encore £9195; Ghia £11,560.

Changes in 1996 had transformed the Fiesta from merely workmanlike into a best-selling class leader. Key ingredients for the Fiesta V Codenamed BE256 were the 1.6 Zetec-S engine which gave sporty Fiestas their ST title, with wheels, tyres, gearbox, and interior changed. Suspension was lowered 13mm (.5in) in front and 10mm (.4in) at the back, the front anti-roll bar thickened by 2mm to 17mm (.7in) and the rear twist beam stiffened 42 per cent, aimed at flatter roll-free cornering. Importantly the steering gained a heavier rack to improve its feel and it reverted to 2.8 turns lock to lock. A fashion fad was a mesh grille over the oval air intake, imitating the wire screens that 1930s sports racing cars wore to protect headlamps and radiator cores from the flying stones, with which racetracks, particularly Le Mans, once abounded.

Entry-level Fiestas meanwhile carried on with much the same mechanicals, Endura petrol and diesel editions chugging on in the basement, 1.25 and 1.4 also remaining mechanically unchanged. What they all gained was a facelift with a lower bonnet line and trapezoidal headlights although trying to disguise all the old presswork was not an unqualified success. So long as basic ingredients of cost, economy, roadworthiness, and proportions were right, however, the rest could look after itself. Efforts at a proper flagship Fiesta had been undistinguished and it took three years to produce another.

ZETEC-S: Oct 1999 to 2002; weight 975kg (2149.5lb); 4-cylinders; 79mm x 81.4mm, 1596cc; 76kW (101.9bhp) @ 6000rpm; 47.6kW (63.8bhp)/l; 145Nm (107lbft) @ 4000rpm. Twin belt-driven ohc, 4-valve; aluminium head, and block; Siemens electronic fuel injection, electronic engine management; 5-bearing crankshaft. 5-speed synchromesh; final drive 4.25:1; traction control. Wheelbase 244.5cm (96.3in); track 143cm (56.3in) front, 137.5cm (54.1in) rear; length 383cm (150.8in); width 163cm (64.2in); height 141cm (55.5in); ground clearance 14cm (5.5in); turning circle 10.3m (33.8ft).15-spoke alloy wheels, CD player; electric front windows;
1.25-litre available with CVT optional £1000; Zetec-S 3-door only. Maximum speed 182kph (113.4mph); 33.7kph (21mph) @ 1000rpm; 0-100kph (62mph) 10.2sec; 12.8kg/kW (9.6kg/bhp); fuel consumption 6.9-6l/100km (40.9-47.1mpg). 1.3 Encore £7750; 1.25LX £9750; 1.4 Zetec £9750; 4-door 1.4 Ghia £11,850.

While normally aspirated and rather noisy Endura D diesels offered comparable power against rivals, they took half a second longer than the Volkswagen Polo to 100kph (62mph) and were around 6kph (4mph)

Freelance Fiesta special edition.
2001 Fiesta Freestyle.

slower. Both used indirect fuel injection, while contemporaries were moving on to direct, some even to new-fangled common rail diesels. Even though Fiestas had power steering, a sunroof, driver's airbag, and a radio that could be upgraded to Radio Data System (RDS) for £60, they had not quite kept pace with the opposition.

Fiesta diesels had still seemed well down the pecking order, until March 2000, when they inherited the turbocharged 1.8 Focus TDdi, which also went into the small Fiesta and Courier panel vans. Performance was on a par with the 1.25 petrol Fiesta, it used less fuel (5.3l/100km (53.3mpg) against 6.1l/100km (46.3mpg), but more importantly it was a match in smooth running and enjoyed a reduction in vibration. The price of the new generation diesel Fiesta was the same as the outgoing model and it came in 5-door form. Option packs to upgrade the specification continued.

Production of the completely new Fiesta V, launched at the Frankfurt Motor Show on 11 September 2001, was not expected to start until the following spring. It brought the still sprightly 25-year-old firmly into the 21st century with a stylish new body shell and more space inside. Fuel costs were still increasing. Environmentalists were demanding results, so together with most cars of the new Millennium, Fiestas achieved what a few years previously would have been regarded as unbelievable.

Replacing Endura E, the petrol 1.3-litre Duratec's combined figure of 6.2l/100km (45.6mpg) was attainable in everyday driving, as was the 1.4 diesel Duratorq's 4.3l/100km (65.7mpg). The Fiesta's driving quality was well received, and it was equipped with the

Shapely Diesel Fiesta of 2006.

IPS intelligent safety system with up to six airbags. The small Duratec 8-valve engine achieved economy by reducing internal friction. The camshaft drive was a roller chain instead of the usual toothed belt, the valve stems were reduced to 6mm (.24in) diameter, and the sophisticated electronic system kept the stoichiometric (petrol and air) mixture so consistent that emissions were controlled better than before. Nearly 90 per cent of maximum pulling power was available between 1500rpm and 4500rpm. A compact engine

5.3cm (2.1in) less than before top to bottom, and 3mm (.12in) shorter end to end, it also featured a new Powertrain Control Module (PCM), electronic throttle control for the first time in a small Ford.

Together with the Ford Street Ka, the 2002 Paris Motor Show featured the 3-door Fiesta that made its UK debut a few weeks later at Birmingham. In Finesse, LX and Zetec trim its sportier sloping roofline and angled tailgate were, Ford claimed, aimed at younger drivers. In fact, it was identical

Two doors and a hatchback. 2002 in red.

to the more upright 5-door below the body crease. To achieve a separate identity the 3-door's roof was lowered from the top of the A-pillar towards the back, and the C-pillar brought forward by 75mm (2.95in), creating something vaguely coupe-like. It meant losing 8mm (.31in) in rear-seat headroom, but by way of compensation there was more stowage in bigger front door bins along with pockets beside the back seat. VDA boot volume was slightly smaller at 268l (9.5cuft) against 284l (10cuft) for the 5-door.

The Fiesta nomenclature was ever adaptable and overlapping. The April 2002 Mark V was sometimes known as Mark VI, because the old Mark IV was sometimes called Mark VI following the 1999 facelift. Fiesta "Classics" were born-again previous years' models to spin out component volumes. The extended Amulssafes Valencia plant, later earmarked for a concentration on electric cars, started making the Mark V Fiesta in April 2002. Its trim lines were Finesse, LX, Zetec, and Ghia along with limited-edition

variants with anti-lock brakes and passenger airbags. Replacing a Kia-based Festiva it became the first Fiesta sold in Australasia and Asia. Valencia also made a supercharged 1 litre car for Brazil, extending exports to Argentina on 2004 and India in 2005.

Fiesta Classics had two engine options; the diesel Duratorq TDCi 1.4-litre, an early product of an agreement between Ford and Peugeot Citroën (PSA) that went back to 1998, or the petrol Duratec 16v 1.4-litre, with electronic, drive-by-wire throttle control. The arrival of the 3-door coincided with Durashift EST (Electronic Shift Technology) an automatic-shift transmission providing the flexibility of a manual with the ease of an automatic. The driver could choose between fully automatic, or a sequential shift, actuated by three electric motors, two changing gears, one operating the clutch.

Durashift EST was to be maintenance-free up to 145,000miles (233,350km). According to Glen Goold, Chief Programme Engineer, "Durashift EST adapted to changing driving

conditions, like hills and curves, making it ideal for drivers who would prefer an automatic but don't want to pay a penalty in performance, feel or fuel economy". The 3-door's weight was 1035kg (2281.8lb), diesel 1065kg (2347.9lb), it had the passive anti-theft system D-PATS and the 1.6 Ghia was priced at £11,195 and TDCi £10,965.

The model won a Golden Steering Wheel from Bild am Sonntag newspaper, but the Durashift EST turned out to be problematic.

A 2004 recreation of the 1981 XR2 and 1989 XR2i, of which British enthusiasts bought 34,000, was not straightforward. The problem facing XR buyers had always been insurance. XR designations raised insurer's hackles, putting premiums up particularly for younger buyers the car was aimed at, so Ford created Team RS.

Sports Technologies (ST) was a sporting sales subdivision which, besides colour-keyed body details, fancy bumpers, rubbing strips, outside mirror finishers and 17in 11-spoke alloy wheels, achieved the Fiesta ST's competitive insurance rating of 13E. Jost Capito, Team RS director: "ST was more than just a badge; it was a whole new performance and design concept." ST was a term carried through to the Fiesta's eventual replacement.

Sports Technologies (ST) Fiestas were also applied to the Focus, with the addition of a 225 PS 2.5-litre 5-cylinder turbocharged engine. Ford was able to draw on designs developed elsewhere within the Premier Automotive Group established by Jacques Nasser that cost $17 billion in 1999 and included Lincoln, Mercury, Aston Martin, Jaguar, and Volvo that sourced an engine not only propelling the ST to 60mph inside 6.5sec, but also into *What Car?'s* honours for 2006 as best hot-hatch against the VW Golf Gti,

Team RS introduced its first car at the 2004 Geneva Motor Show, putting it on sale in January 2005 as a 150PS Fiesta with a vigorous 2-litre engine and chassis tuning to provide handling matching its speed. Racing style seats were trimmed in black leather with bold red centre sections bearing an ST logo. A leather steering wheel and metal pedals completed the sporty picture and by the time the car reached buyers in 2005, the rear spoiler was altered to achieve less drag

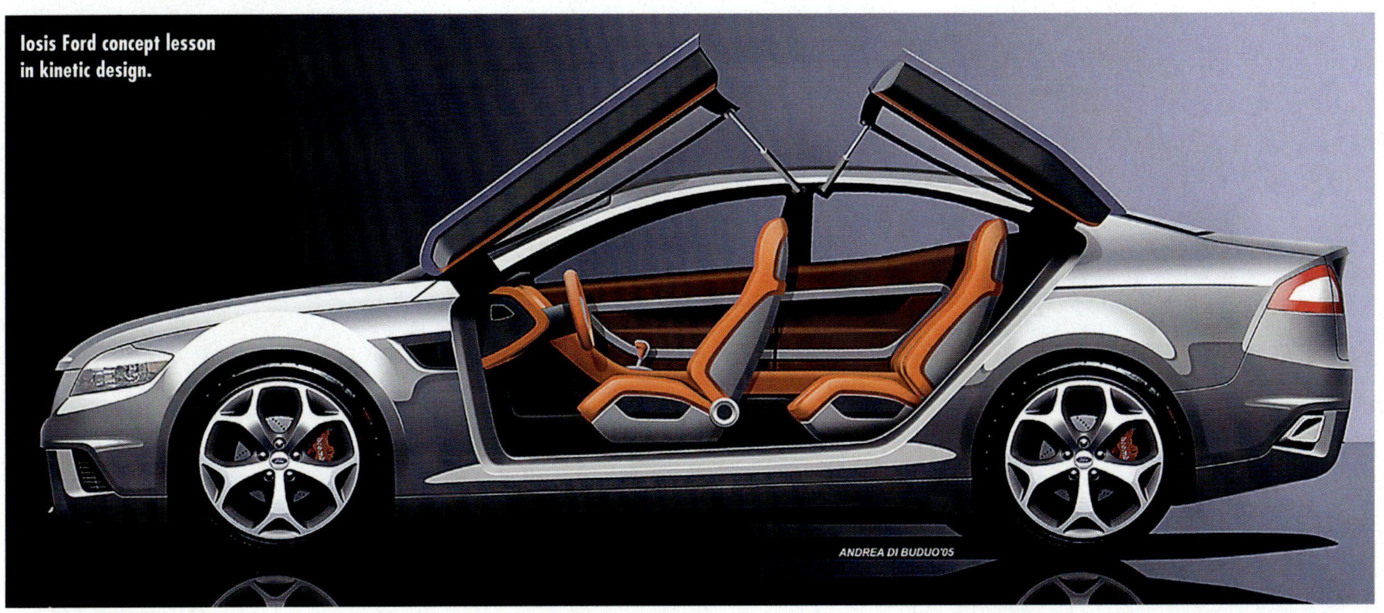

Verve concept at Frankfurt Motor Show 2007.

Chequered roof for Fiesta Zetec S Celebration.

and more downforce, the steering ratio was raised, and the seats were more supportive.

Later in 2004, with more enthusiasts appreciating the ambitious torque of modern turbo-diesels, it was time for the Fiesta Zetec S, which shared some of the dynamics and cosmetics of the ST, including discreet side skirts and the rear spoiler on the roof trailing edge, with the 1.6 TDCi engine. The Zetec S was also available with the 1.6 16-valve petrol engine, and a choice of four colours including an exclusive Magnum Grey metallic. Twin body stripes were optional at £150, side stripes £75. STs could do 208kph (129.5mph), TDCis 179.8kph (112mph), ST 0-100kph (62mph) 8.4sec, TDCi 11.2sec, 1.6 petrol 9.9sec. ST fuel consumption 5.7l/100km (49.6mpg), prices ST £13,595; TDCi £12,495; Zetec S petrol £11,595.

New editions at Frankfurt in 2001 amounted to little more than new bumpers and grille, new headlamps and rear lamps, thicker body side mouldings, body-coloured handles and mirrors on "selected models". A new facia and better materials with a "soft feel" upper section made up some of the ground lost to competitors. The interior was a little more daring, but not much.

In autumn 2004 along with new engines, the Fiesta 3-door and 5-door were given what Ford called a designer makeover for Model Year 2006. This sixth generation code-named variously B299 and B409 in 2008 under the global B-car platform could be known as Mark VI or VII in the UK. It was shown at Frankfurt in September 2007 as the Ford Verve Concept hinting at a new approach for compact cars. As ever Ford was testing public reaction to guide designers working on the next supermini and followed Iosis and Iosis X, with what Martin Smith, Executive Director of Design called the kinetic philosophy behind Mondeo and S-MAX. It would be, bold, radical, "…a small car that is a chic and modern, and one that makes an individual statement for a sophisticated, fashion-aware generation." The front of Verve was dominated by a large, inverted trapezoidal lower grille with the Ford oval centre-stage.

Verve was shown in deep magenta with a tinted clear coat finish, 18in alloy wheels, panoramic glass roof and B-pillarless structure to give it a coupe-like look. Inside it was inspired by the latest mobile phones' curviness and

was part of a global policy closer to what was known as the "One Ford" strategy that had prompted policy at Dearborn ever since the time of the Fiesta's launch. Production of the new generation began in Cologne and Valencia 2008, then in succeeding years at assembly plants in China, Thailand, Mexico and Brazil. At the 2012 Paris Motor Show, it became the first with the common trapezoidal grille.

What Ford called the Global Product Development System (GPDS) was established and more followed. Adjustments could be made to meet different countries' requirements, better ride and handling to suit European driving, for example and important innovations were made in engines. Better fuel economy and emissions were crucial during increasingly ecologically charged times. Emissions of CO_2 were reduced by over 11,000 tonnes against previous Fiestas. There was an ultra-low CO_2 ECOnetic model with emissions of 98g/km and a top range 1.6-litre Duratec Ti-VCT petrol. Improvements to responsiveness, economy and emissions came through improvements to 1.4 and 1.6litre Duratorq TDCi diesels. Electric power assisted steering was something of a token gesture to greenery, as well as avoiding the expense and complication of hydraulics.

Fiestas remained worthy. Many testers reckoned it the best-handling supermini and it was rated highly for practicality. Space inside was generous, the constant increases in size over previous models especially in the back, met buyers' demands. The growing aspirational popularity of Sports Utility Vehicles (SUVs) cast a long shadow, and although the boot was not large it was a good shape for square luggage. The diesels earned most praise, 1.25 and 1.4 petrol cars gained more credit for economy than speed.

To try and maintain British sales at 100,000 (along with Fusion) for the year, a number of features were added, including rain sensing wipers, automatic "home safe" headlight mode, air conditioning, one touch driver's electric window, and MP3-compatible stereo. The Fiesta came joint top with the Nissan Micra in *What Car?*'s security tests that proved burglars unable to break through the fixed allocation of deadlocks inside two minutes.

The 2004 Fiesta ST, the return
of the hot-hatch?

Fiesta's smile seemed to widen with sales records in 2004.

A long series of limited edition versions came in with the 30th anniversary Zetec S. Launched in Radian Yellow with chequered roof, it was followed from April 2006 by a special edition of 2,500 Fiesta Freedoms. They launched an £800 package of extras of voice command, mobile phone, satellite navigation and music technology of which Mark Ovenden, marketing director, Ford of Britain said: "Mobile phone use has increased dramatically in Britain in the last five years and this generation wants connectivity in all areas of their life. Fiesta Freedom is the ultimate hands-free accessory and I'm sure there will be plenty of buyers who decide to take the long route home while they enjoy flicking around their CD collection or having an extra chat – without lifting a finger. Vodafone is a natural partner for the small car that most people choose in Britain's car dealerships. With more than 13 million customers in the UK, Vodafone too are well placed to provide the most up-to-date product for customers who want an excellent product with a stylish look."

The Fiesta Freedom had a choice of 1.25 or 1.4 litre engines, 3 or 5-doors and for the first time in a small Ford Bluetooth technology to handle phone calls, voice control for radio channels and CD selection with thousands of MP3 tracks. Buyers could sign up to a special deal with Vodafone from £25 a month for a G3 Nokia N70 phone, cradle and Tom Tom Mobile 5 satellite navigation viewed through the phone inside or outside the car.

Unique 15in alloy wheels, heated body-coloured mirrors, body-coloured door and tailgate handles and front fog lights, with unique 'Freedom' badge on the tailgate, it had remote central double locking, remote tailgate release, electric front windows, rear spoiler, leather steering wheel with aluminium trim and silver trim on dashboard. *Ford*

FROM NOVEMBER 2005: Saloon; 3 or 5-doors, 5-seats; weight 1.4, 1030kg (2270.7lb), 1.25 1100kg (2425lb), 1.6 1040kg (2292.8lb), TDCi1060kg (2336.9lb). 4-cylinders, front; transverse; 71.9mm x 76.5mm; 1242cc: compression 10.1:1; 55kW (73.8bhp) @ 6000rpm; 44.3kW (59.4bhp)/l; 110Nm (81.1lbft) @ 4000rpm. 74 x 75.5mm; 1299cc; cr 10.2:1; 51kW (68.4bhp) @ 5600rpm; 39.2kW (52.6bhp)/l; 106Nm (18.2lbft) @ 2600rpm. 76mm x 76.5mm, 1388cc; cr 11:1; 59kW (79.1bhp) @ 5700rpm; 42.5kW (56.9bhp)/l; 124Nm (91.4lbft) @ 3500rpm. 79mm x 81.4mm; 1596cc; 74kW (99.2bhp) @ 6000rpm; 46.4kW (62.2bhp)/l; 146Nm (107.7lbft) @ 4000rpm, or 84kW (112.6bhp) @ 6000rpm; 52.6kW (70.5bhp)/l; 155Nm (114lbft) @ 4150rpm. 87.5 x 83.1mm, 1.4TDCi 73.7mm x 82mm; 1399cc; compr 17.9:1; 50kW (67.1bhp) @ 4000rpm; 35.7kW (47.9bhp)/l; 160Nm (118lbft) @ 2000rpm. 1.6 TDCi 75mm x 88.3mm; 1560cc; cr 18:1; 80kW (107.3bhp) @ 4000rpm; 51.3kW (68.8bhp)/l; 204Nm (150.5lbft) @ 1750rpm. 1.25 and 1.6 petrol 16-valves; 2 belt-driven ohc; aluminium head, block; fuel inj, Siemens electronic engine management; 5-brg crank. 1.3 8-valve 2 belt-driven ohc; TDCi 1.4 8-valves 1 chain driven ohc, 1.6 16-valves, 2 chain-driven ohc; aluminium. Front wheel drive; hydraulic sdp clutch; 5-speed synchromesh manual gearbox; final drive 3.37:1 1.4, 1.25, 4.25:1, 1.6, 4.25 and 4.28; TDCi 1.4 3.37:1. Steel monocoque; ifs by MacPherson struts, offset coil spring, lower arms on subframe, rear torsion beam axle; telescopic dampers; anti-roll bar; hydraulic vacuum servo split dual circuit, 25.8cm (10.2in) ventilated front disc and drum brakes, ABS; PAS; 43l (9.5gal) tank;195/60R15, 195/55R16 tyres 6J rims. Wheelbase 248.5cm (97.8in); track front 147.5cm (58.1), rear 144.5cm (56.9in); length 391.5cm (154.1in); width 168cm (66.1in); height 146cm (57.5in); ground clearance 14cm (5.5in); turning circle 10.3m (33.8ft). Rain-sensing wipers; optional satellite navigation; MP3 connection. Maximum speed 1.3 160kph (99.6mph), 1.25 163kph (101.5mph), 1.4 166kph (103.4mph), 1.6 TDCi 180kph (112.1mph); 34.8kph (21.7mph) @ 1000rpm, 1.4 34.5kph (21.5mph), 1.6 TDCi 42.8kph (26.7mph); 0-100kph (62mph) 17.3sec, 1.4 13.2sec, 1.6 TDCi 11.9sec; fuel consumption (mean official figs) 6.24l/100km (45.2mpg), 1.4 6.4l/100km (44.1mpg); 1.4TDCi 4.33l/100km (65.1mpg). 1.25 16v Studio 3-door £8,395; 1.6 Ghia 5-door £12,545; 1.6 TDCi £12,495.

SUBSCRIBE
TO YOUR FAVOURITE MAGAZINE
AND SAVE

Classic Land Rover is an exciting monthly magazine dedicated to Series and the classic Land Rovers. Written by enthusiasts, it is the complete guide to buying, owning, running, driving, repairing, modifying, and restoring pre-nineties Land Rovers and Range Rover classics.

Classiclandrover.com

Ka concept. A flyer to see what it was worth.

KA: THE MINIATURE FIESTA

The production technology that enabled the Ka was an important ingredient of its style. Chris Clements, head designer admitted that five years ago, Ka would not have been contemplated because body-press techniques could not guarantee the knife-edge fits and close-cut shut-lines that exemplified "origami". Its shape was an ingenious mixture of fluid curves and near-flat panels, continuous lines between practical polypropylene mouldings below the waistline, and sheet steel upper portions providing exquisite balance. The proportions were exemplary, the wide-tracked, wheel-at-each-corner stance a masterpiece of former Royal College of Art student Chris Svensson. The production Ka was crisper than the roly-poly prototype at Geneva of 1994 and had the further virtue of cutting 25% off a Fiesta's build time.

The Ka was as wide as a Fiesta, yet slightly taller, with more head room and shoulder space. There were two equipment levels, Ka and Ka2 and only one engine option, the old pushrod Endura-E that was light and cheap. The interior was just as radical; the facia had sweeping curves and although in reality quite basic, looked stylish and well-resourced. Cars with power steering had 2.9 turns lock to lock instead of 4.2, different castor angles, fatter tyres and shorter gearing satisfying PAS buyers who wanted different driving qualities.

Clay modellers work on Ka facia designs.

The modellers' result. Ka facia.

1996 KA: 3-doors, 4-seats; weight 870kg (1918lb). 4-cylinders, transverse; 75mm x 75.5mm, 1299cc; compr 8.8:1; 44kW (59bhp) @ 5000rpm; 33.9kW (45.4bhp)/l; 103Nm (76lbft) @ 2500rpm. Pushrod ohv; chain-driven camshaft, cast iron cylinder head and block; Ford EEC-V electronic sequential fuel injection and engine management; 5-bearing crankshaft. Front wheel drive; 5-speed synchromesh; final drive 4.06:1. Steel monocoque; ifs by MacPherson strut, offset coil springs, lower A-arms, anti-roll bar; rear suspension semi-independent twist beam with coil spring damper units; hydraulic servo brakes, front 24cm (9.5in) disc, rear drums, ABS optional; rack and pinion, optional PAS; 42l (9.2 gal) tank; 165/65R13 tyres, 5J rims. Wheelbase 245cm (96.5in); track 139.5cm (54.9in) front, 141cm (55.5in) rear; length 362cm (142.5in); width 164cm (64.6in); height 140cm (55.1in); ground clearance 14cm (5.5in); turning circle 10.3m (33.8ft). Rear wash-wipe, driver's airbag, radio/cassette player standard, passenger airbag, air conditioning and alloy wheels option; Ka2 PAS electric windows standard. Maximum speed 155kph (96.6mph); 32.4kph (20.2mph) @ 1000rpm; 0-100kph (62mph) 15.4sec; 19.8kg/kW (14.7kg/bhp); 6.7l/100km (42.2mpg). Price £7350; Ka2 £8195.

StreetKa Blue Edition 2002.

A StreetKa roadster had been a concept at the Turin Motor Show in 2000. Public and press reaction to it was good, and in Geneva the following spring Ford confirmed that it would go into production, with the Duratec 1.6 8-valve engine.

Designed by David Willkie of the Turin Ghia Studio, it was turned into a production reality, ironically by Ghia's old rival Industrie Pininfarina SpA. Under Wilkie's supervision Pininfarina engineered it for volume production and launch in 2003. "We drew crowds whenever we showed it," said Martin Leach, Ford of Europe's vice president of product development. Ford was trying to find a new way of reaching customers unconnected from motor sport yet exemplifying the nature of the Ford range, so StreetKa teamed up with Kylie Minogue as a sponsor of her 39-date 2002 European Fever Tour, from Cardiff to Barcelona. The production StreetKa featured in photographs with Kylie, providing a preview before it went on sale in 2003. "The partnership with Kylie was the perfect way to show off the StreetKa ahead of its launch," said Peter Fleet, marketing director. "The StreetKa and Kylie had a lot in common; they were both small, beautiful and stylish." The car was formally unveiled to the public at the Paris Motor Show in September 2002.

COUPE: 2-doors, 4-seats; weight 1061kg (2339.1lb). 4-cylinders, transverse; 82.07 x 75.48mm; 1597cc; compr 9.5:1; 70kW (93.9bhp) @ 5500rpm; 43.8kW (58.8bhp)/l; 135Nm (100lbft) @ 4250rpm. Duratec 8V; chain-driven overhead camshaft; 2-valves; aluminium cylinder head, iron block;

Street KA Limited Edition.

SportKa on test.

Ka a million.

sequential multipoint electronic fuel injection, Siemens integrated engine management, distributorless electronic ignition; 5-bearing 4-counterweight crankshaft. Front wheel drive; hydraulic single plate diaphragm spring clutch; gearbox 5-speed synchromesh; final drive 4.25:1 Steel monocoque; independent front suspension by MacPherson struts with offset spring-damper units, lower arms on separate cross-member; anti-roll bar; semi-independent rear suspension twist-beam, coil springs; telescopic dampers; hydraulic servo brakes dual circuit diagonally split, front 25.8cm (10.16in) ventilated discs, rear 20.3cm (8in) drums, 4-channel ABS optional on left hand drive; rack and pinion PAS; 42l (9.2gal) tank; 195/45R16tyres, 5J rims six-spoke alloy wheels. Wheelbase 244.8cm (96.4in); track front 141.7cm (55.8in), rear 145.2cm (57.2in); length 365cm (143.7in); width 169.5cm (66.7in); height 133.5cm (52.6in); ground clearance 14cm (5.5in); turning circle 11.1m (36.4ft). Ford 6000 RDS/EON two-channel radio/CD player; air conditioning, leather upholstery optional. Maximum speed 173kph (108mph); 0-100kph (62mph) 12.1sec; 15.2kg/kW (11.3kg/bhp); fuel consumption 7.9l/100km (35.8mpg).

When Ka sales exceeded a million, the StreetKa roadster and SportKa brought the range to three. Brentwood could not resist "zesty" and "sparkling" when the SportKa was first exposed at the Paris Motor Show in the autumn of 2002, the launch coinciding with Ford America's centenary year. The "coolest Ka" had lower, stiffer springing with different toe-in and camber and a South African-made engine with a close-ratio gearbox. Identified by flared wheel arches, and 16in instead of 13in alloy wheels with low-profile tyres, together with a sporty spoiler

A Sport Ka named desire.

blending into the wrap-round rear bumper, the Sport had the Street's curious central round reversing light and the option of unique Imperial Blue paintwork.

Sportka adopted a similar grille and body-coloured front bumper, and among features borrowed from the soon to be discontinued Puma, was its unusual aluminium ball gearshift. More resistance to body roll was achieved by a 64 per cent increase in anti-roll bar firmness and the front spring rates were 30 per cent higher. Rear roll stiffness on the Fiesta's twist-beam rear suspension

was 45 per cent more and rear spring rates went up seven per cent. The 8-valve Duratec delivered 90 per cent of its torque between 1500-4500rpm and also met Euro Stage IV emission regulations. A 1.3 70PS version was available in some markets. It was priced in the UK at £10,295; SE £11,295.

Radical when it first appeared in 1996, Ka's origami style proved successful, with a useful increase in the volume lowering the cost of its Fiesta underpinnings. Its numbers would barely have justified it as a stand-alone model however, so when a replacement was

due Ford and Fiat found common cause, co-producing two models on the same basis. Ka's days on its own were numbered.

After the Millennium there was a lot of car industry crossbreeding. It had been years since manufacturers of aircraft coalesced into a handful of firms and car makers were following suit. Suzuki made 12,000 Mitsubishis, the 1.5litre Maven for Indonesia. Fiat and Suzuki made a medium-sized Sports Utility Vehicle that came to market not only as a Fiat but also a new sort of Lancia. The Suzuki Grand Vitara dispensed with its co-

Driver's view of Ka.

Compact Ka instruments.

Ka Collection. 2008.

Ka cutaway to show
Fiesta ancestry.

Ford publicity picture labelled "Fiesta".

London bridge lights Ka 2008.

Ford publicity picture labelled "Ka".

operative PSA Peugeot-Citroën diesel engine, to use one made by Renault. PSA signed a deal with Mitsubishi to develop another SUV.

Fiat's Polish plant at Tychy had been making Pandas since 2003. Its output reached 360,000 in 2007 with the introduction of the Fiat 500. Now Fiat and Ford started making a Ka-sized minicar, starting at 100,000 a year, the same design with different upperworks to distinguish the different marques. It was much like the multiparty minicar made at Kolín in the Czech Republic by PSA and Toyota. Structure, platform, parts and sub-assemblies were identical yet different bodies identified them as Peugeots, Citroëns and Toyotas. Kolín made 300,000 cars a year; 200,000 Peugeots and Citroëns, 100,000 Toyotas.

Adding the Ka, with its Fiesta connections, took Tychy's production to over half a million, making the factory viable and competitive. Ironically the original Bobcat project of 1976 had used the Fiat 127 as a role model so there was a logic behind it. Ford's version of the Tychy car was probably better, changes to the suspension and steering improved its ride and handling. *Autocar* columnist Steve Cropley had no doubts: "Ford needs to embody modern design values, not pick up a lot of retro cues like the Fiat. Ford has amassed a great reputation for providing some of the best-handling mainstream cars, but it has never been required to use someone else's suspension. Ford insiders confirmed that they examined the Fiat hardware (while it was in the very last design stages) and satisfied themselves that it could work under a Ford." *What Car?* magazine confirmed Cropley's confidence: "It's nimble through corners and accurate to steer. The ride is surprisingly good for such a small car – more settled than the Fiat."

Ford's empire now stretched into a joint venture in Thailand and China, through alliances with Changan Ford and Jiangling Motors. Companies assembling Ford models included Pininfarina Italy, Santana Spain, Otosan and Otokar in Turkey, and pieces of Fords were made by technical alliances with Getrag factories in France, Germany, and the UK.

The Ka's relaunch at the Paris Motor Show in August 2008 hailed by Ford as, "Fresh, funky and fun, bold, fashionable and stylish. Full of youthful and cheeky Ka spirit. An exciting successor to the iconic original. New levels of style and enjoyment to affordable city cars. Twelve years after the original Ka was launched to great acclaim, its successor captures the same youthful and cheeky spirit. The new model retains all of the qualities which made the Ka so popular – its compact size, great looks, lively dynamics and fun personality – but presents them in a fresh new package."

It had been given a new appearance based around the kinetic design form language and it was well received unlike the Ecosport two years later. *Ford*

2009 KA. Saloon; 3-doors, 4-seats; weight 865kg (1907lb), 1.3TDCi 980kg (2160.5lb). 4-cylinders, transverse; 70.8mm x 78.9mm, 1242cc; compr 11.1:1; 51kW (68.4bhp) @ 5500rpm; 41kW (55bhp)/l; 102Nm (75.2lbft) @ 3000rpm. 1.3 69.6 x 82; 1248cc; compr 17.6:1; 55 kW (73.8bhp) @4000rpm; 145Nm (106.9lbft) @ 3500rpm; 2-valves; belt driven ohc; aluminium head, block; fuel injection; 5-bearing crankshaft. 1.3, 2 chain-driven ohc; direct injection, turbocharger, intercooler. Front wheel drive; hydraulic sdp clutch; 5-speed synchromesh; final drive 3.44:1. Steel monocoque; MacPherson strut ifs; anti-roll bar; rear folded sheet steel torsion beam axle; telescopic dampers; anti roll bar; hydraulic servo brakes, front 24cm (9.4in) disc, rear 18cm (7in) drums, ABS, EBD; r&p electric PAS; 35l (7.7gal) tank; 175/65 R14, 195/50 R15 tyres, 5.5, 6J rims. 1.3 ventilated discs. Wheelbase 230cm (90.5in); track front 141cm (55.5in), rear 140cm (55.1in); length 362cm (142.5in); width 166cm (65.4in); height 150.5cm (59.2in). 1.3, 151cm (59.4in). Air conditioning on Edge, Zetec, Titanium; optional ESP. Maximum speed 159kph (98.8mph); 0-100kph (62mph) 13.1sec; fuel consumption 5l/100km (55.4mpg). 1.3 4.2l/100km (67.3mpg). Studio £7995, 1.3 Zetec £10,195.

Iosis SUV concept Frankfurt.

FUSION AND ECOSPORT
FIESTA FOUNDLINGS

The Fusion concept at the 2001 Frankfurt Motor Show wore the customary aspect of an off-road adventure vehicle embarking on a safari. At Geneva six months later, in production form, it emerged as a practical highly adaptable mini-MPV, with five seats that could be folded flat to provide the load space of an estate car several sizes bigger. With ample compartments for maps, picnic items, and family paraphernalia, the Fusion was a versatile small car on the Fiesta platform, with all the Fiesta's roadworthiness and refinement. The obligation for a volume car manufacturer to produce as many variations as possible on one overall concept, namely the Fiesta, brought Ford into a diverse, flourishing market.

The Frankfurt Fusion's turbocharged direction-injection petrol engine with Variable Cam Timing (VCT), automated Durashift Electronic Select Transmission, navigation system with telematics and integrated multi-media entertainment system was not carried through to production. Instead, the Geneva car was an Urban Activity Vehicle (UAV)

with a sensible choice of TDCi common rail turbodiesel, or two 16-valve petrol engines. With its tall body, easy to get in and out of, and clever detailing like a front passenger seat that folded into a table, the Fusion provided taxi-like maneuverability, along with roominess for the urban dweller, within the footprint of a compact car.

Diesel technology advanced a step with development of the ohc 2-valve 44kW (59bhp) engine from the 1996 Fiesta for the Ford Focus. Direct injection into the combustion chambers rather than the inlet tract, together with precise electronic metering, turbocharger and intercooler, added 23kW (30.8bhp). Emissions were reduced and direct injection also raised the torque over earlier versions by 11 per cent, so it pulled strongly between 1500 and 3600rpm, until the fuel cutoff point at 4800rpm. Once the turbocharger was integrated into the exhaust manifold it was also more economical and refined. Oil-filled engine mountings and fixings for the exhaust, well outside the floor area of the cabin, were further enhancements.

In 2001 the diesel was brought completely up-to-date with the Duratorq TDCi common-rail version that averaged 4.4l/100km (65mpg) and was expected to save its owner £300 in fuel costs before the time of its first service. Routine maintenance was claimed to cost 28 per cent less than the previous Fiesta after service intervals were increased to 20,000km (12,500miles). Bumpers were strengthened and bolt-on wings made repairs cheaper. A CO_2 rating of only 119g./km was significant in view of a new tax structure, introduced to the UK in April 2002, which took account of vehicle emissions.

The Fiesta reached maturity with a glowing reputation for space and practicality, yet some disappointment perhaps over the cabin materials, low-speed ride, and refinement. Most drivers turned out to be perfectly happy to trade a bit of firm springing for good road grip and safe, enjoyable handling. The engine range was wide: 1.3 8-valve; 1.25 16-valve; 1.4, 1.4TDCi and 1.6 16-valve. Furthermore, the Fiesta retained its good name for safety and security equipment, with

the customary standard passenger airbags and antilock brakes.

Fusion gained some cosmetic enhancements at the 2003 Geneva Motor Show and was called Fusion Plus by Spring 2005. For only the second time on a UK Ford it had DVD rear seat entertainment; it gained an extra 10.7l (0.38cuft) stowage space and the optional Electronic Stability Programme (ESP). The DVD's infra-red headsets eliminated tangled cables, and the system functioned for half an hour after the car was switched off before shutting down to preserve battery life. Fusion had three engine choices, the 1.4-litre 68PS TDCi, 1.4-litre 80PS and 1.6-litre 100PS 16v. Small-engined Fiestas were manual 5-speeds. The 1.4L and 1.4TDCi could have manual or EST advanced manual and for 2004 both Fusion and Fiesta gained a new fully automatic transmission for the 1.6 16v, a conventional 4-speed with hydraulic clutches, brakes and planetary gears. The third generation high-pressure common rail diesel 90PS Duratorq 1.6L TDCi joined the existing 68PS 1.4 8-valve to take Fiesta and Fusion into the growing "premium diesel" sub segment. This accounted for nearly a quarter of B class sales in the UK, Germany, France and Spain.

Bluetooth hands-free technology, relaying a caller's voice over the car speakers when the hands-free phone was in use, was one of the Fusion's features for model year 2006. Sales were pushed at dealerships to sustain what was, in effect, a taller multi-purpose Fiesta that had more space, a higher driving position and good visibility. The Fiesta and Fusion together were Britain's third best-selling model and second-best supermini to the Vauxhall Corsa. Like all Fiesta based Fords, from the Puma to the Ka, it was good to drive, even though it was putting on weight.

Updated colours came in for the new season, with the trip computer counting miles down to empty, average and actual fuel consumption, average speed, trip distance and outside temperature. Tech-savvy customers were expecting more and more data. Optional air conditioning had automatic temperature control. Powered and heated mirrors folded away when the central locking was activated, or they could be moved away manually for parking in tight spaces. Fusion had a choice of two petrol and two diesel engines, 5-speed gearbox, or two automatic transmissions. The comprehensive list of options could be rationalised into packs; Reflex (side thorax airbags, side air-curtain airbags and centre rear head restraint, together with Electronic Stability Programme ESP). Interior styling included colour co-ordinated mats and appliqué features. Smokers could specify an ashtray and cigar lighter.

ECOSPORT

A sports utility body on the Fiesta platform at the Amsterdam Motor Show in 2012 must have looked like a good idea, a small SUV. The style and space of big SUVs was making them aspirational and Ecosport now spread that out to small family car buyers looking to follow suit at lower cost. It aimed to combine agility affordability and fuel efficiency, with the bigger car's attributes, however, squeezing all that into a B-platform package was not going to be easy. Built firstly at the Chennai plant in India, it looked promising against rivals like Nissan's Juke, selling in decent numbers, with various updates over the years, yet its reception in the press was consistently lukewarm.

Even though, Nick Collins, B-car vehicle line director Ford of Europe, thought: "EcoSport great value for quality and fuel economy and present customers with a fantastic small car choice," testers were generally underwhelmed. EcoSport had been developed in South America as a Ford global model that created its own segment in Brazil. It sold more than 700,000 before it was brought to Europe for what Ford saw as an increasing demand for small sports utilities, a segment expected to double over the following five years. There were buyers who liked the style and price of full-sized SUVs but were unconcerned over lacking four-wheel drive. It was to be followed by the B-MAX, a compact multi-activity vehicle as well as a new Fiesta.

EcoSport looked robust, with a tall front grille, pretty detailing and outdoorsy cladding on the side sills and bumpers. Its appeal was a tall driving position with a clear view, although the interior was mostly familiar and Fiesta-like, less adventurous than might have been expected given the strong exterior lines. Critics thought it lacked the pizzazz of the Renault Captur.

Ford concepts. Fiesta Focus Ghia of 1992.

It did well on practicality. Headroom and legroom were good, boot space was 310 litres convertible to 1238 litres by folding and tumbling both elements of the 60:40 split rear bench. Mounting the spare wheel on the rear door was a clever way of gaining boot space but seemed a design-led gimmick and made the side-hinged door quite heavy; awkward while grappling with luggage or shopping bags.

The extra weight and frontal area of SUV style made it a lot slower than a Fiesta. Zero to 60mph was taking a leisurely 13 seconds against the ordinary Fiesta at around 10. Yet, while on twisty roads, the EcoSport had little body roll and, "cornered with a precision that's quite pleasing for a supermini-on-stilts. It could even feel a deft performer were it not for light and not particularly engaging steering, presumably set-up to focus on town centres" according to *Autocar*.

Ford's strategy was to keep it simple. A limited range of engines were offered to begin with, the only gearbox option a 5-speed manual. However, a 6-speed Powershift dual-clutch automatic transmission came the following year on the 1.5 litre petrol variant. Early EcoSports were not overburdened with extras. They came in Titanium trim, with the option of upgrading to Titanium X which cost another £1000 and added full leather, cruise control and 17in

The Fiesta and Focus, best-selling best mates.

2014 Ecosport: Fiesta underneath Mini SUV on top.

Ecosport with Jeep carry-over rear spare wheel.

Ecosport interior started out workmanlike.

alloys in place of the standard 16in ones. Ford expected half of EcoSport buyers to choose the X but beyond that, there were few cost options; Sync connectivity package (£250), metallic paint (£495) and rear parking sensors (£210).

Improvements were made and the sales team made a decent fist of it, but in 2018 *Autocar* magazine complained, "This is the new Ecosport, which appears broadly similar to the model it replaces, but Ford has work to do if it is to capitalise on the vast sales potential of the UK supermini SUV segment. How much work? Rather a lot, truth be told. Consider that the opening gambit of our road test verdict on the original 'global' Ecosport put upon us in 2014 and built on the same platform as the Fiesta: 'It's a been a long time since a new Ford was as bad as this'. It wasn't a judgment we took pleasure in, but the interior felt cheap in a way contrary to the asking price, and when it came to handling and ride, this was a car beset with incurable problems. Flat-footed while at the same time lacking grip, the chassis was criminally under-damped, falling well below the often industry-leading standards set by Ford. Performance was merely adequate at best."

It was not until Model Year 2018 when the Ecosport gained four-wheel-drive that it could be taken seriously into the realms of small SUVs. "Ford has sold more than 166,000 EcoSport compact SUVs in Europe since we first introduced it to the region in 2014. Sales have grown 40 per cent," according to Steven Armstrong, group vice president and president, Europe Middle East and Africa. "The new Ford EcoSport offers customers even more style, comfort, capability and choice – blending rugged SUV functionality with city car practicality."

The segment had grown. Registrations went up by more than 21 per cent a year and accounted for more than a quarter of all new passenger cars in 2016, Ford's share going up more than 30 per cent. In the UK alone over 40,000 had been sold since 2013, seven in every ten of them a Titanium. There were styling changes, a 1.5 litre diesel Ford called EcoBlue, new colours, a sporty ST-Line version, more electronics including a floating 8in touch screen for giving commands, cruise control with an adjustable speed limiter and a rear-view camera for reversing. Production now came from Craiova, Romania, joining Ford Edge, and Kuga SUVs and anticipating a Fiesta Active Crossover model in 2019.

Its "intelligent" four-wheel-drive measured how much grip each wheel was achieving, adjusting within 20 milliseconds torque proportionately up to 50/50 between fronts and rears. It provided a sure footing in slippery conditions. The EcoBlue diesel 4-cylinder passed 125PS and 300Nm of torque with a low-inertia turbocharger to a 6-speed manual gearbox.

Even more notably Ecosport gained 140 PS and 125 PS versions of Ford's clever 1.0 litre EcoBoost petrol engine delivering 5.2 l/100 km fuel efficiency and 119 g/km CO_2 emissions. From mid-2018, a 100 PS 1.0-litre EcoBoost model came with a 6-speed manual gearbox. *Autocar* was still not impressed: "The ride is composed, with only the most significant of road ruts communicating to

Black grille and black top enhanced
Ecosport's SUV credentials.

the driver. The EcoBoost engine emits its now-familiar three-pot thrum, noticeable but not overbearing during acceleration and at motorway speeds. Those used to the Fiesta might notice a touch more road and wind noise, but it's not intrusive."

Ford claimed EcoSport had genuine off-roading capability, with 180mm of ground clearance although testers had to wait. *Autocar* did not have the opportunity to test the claim since the lack of the four-wheel-drive variant in the UK model range suggested, "… the only jungle this model will be seen in is an urban one." Fuel consumption was around 40mpg, the 1.5 litre diesel version that cost a premium of £500 returning 45mpg.

EcoSport was competitive in relation to its main rivals, except perhaps the budget-priced Dacia Duster, also from a Romanian factory, although this was a segment where buyers tended to be led by design appeal than a cheap sticker price. In such a competitive market the EcoSport succeeded eventually through an agreeable driving experience, good urban manners, and lots of interior space. Ford EcoSport 1.0 Ecoboost £15,995, 0-62mph 12.7sec. Maximum speed 112mph, 53.3mpg CO2 125g/km, weight 1350kg, 3-cylinders, 999cc, turbocharged, petrol, 123bhp at 6000rpm, torque 125lb ft at 1400-4500rpm.

It wasn't long before the Fiesta had to join the SUV trendiness. The 2018 Fiesta Active had a high driving position and a Range Rover-esque appearance expected to appeal to 15 per cent of Fiesta buyers. The chunky look was extended to Ka+ and Focus as well. Fiesta Actives had plastic wheel arches, extra bumper trim, roof rails and a ride height raised by 1.8cm and track widened by 1cm by way of confirming the 'outdoorsiness' was not all purely cosmetic.

Ford nodded towards the customary outdoors design cues to signify aspirations it described as for an adventurous character. This one had a wide upper grille with strong vertical strakes in gloss black with taller, more prominent side vents reflecting what it called the Active's taller, crossover stance. Seven new alloy wheel designs complemented the bold new styling, and two new exterior colours were available – Boundless Blue and Beautiful Berry.

For the highest level of design and exclusivity, Vignale packs for Titanium, ST-Line and Active series delivered unique design features including exclusive 17 and 18in alloy wheels, premium Sensico seat materials and matte carbon-effect interior decorative elements.

With the SUV boom showing no signs of stopping, by 2019 Ford was not only selling full-sized SUVs with the Kuga, but also jacked-up Active versions of the Focus, Tourneo Connect and Ka+ city car before turning to the Fiesta. The Fiesta Active had a higher ride height and like the unloved Ecosport roof rails and cladding around the wheel arches to make it look countrified. In most other respects it was standard Fiesta and a bit smaller than the competition, the SEAT Arona, Renault Captur, Peugeot 2008 and Citroen C3 Aircross.

There were two trim levels Active Edition based on the regular Fiesta Titanium with sat nav, cruise control and trinkets, as well as Active X Edition with more by way of keyless entry and a B&O sound system. There was only one engine, the 1.0 EcoBoost 3-cylinder with a choice of power outputs, 123 or 153bhp versions, with mild-hybrid technology to reduce fuel consumption, the former with a seven-speed dual-clutch automatic or the standard-fit 6-speed manual. Active Edition was also offered with a non-hybrid 99bhp.

The ride height was 1.8cm taller, which was not much, but the track was widened by 1cm, which made its feet a little more firmly planted on the road, although it changed the feel of a Fiesta very little. Ford expected 15 per cent of the Fiestas it sold to be Active, it was more expensive, but had plusher trim and up-to-date 8in Sync 3 infotainment system. There was no four-wheel-drive option, but it had drive modes that changed the stability programme and allowed a bit more slip on gravelly tracks.

Autocar testers thought it gave a sense of security, doesn't quite replicate a proper 4x4, "… but it gets you a small part of the way there: to a puddle and pothole-strewn car park from where you walk the dogs or, if your lifestyle replicates the advertising campaigns, go kitesurfing or mountain biking. Or it just makes it easier to get in and out in the GP surgery car park (a scenario that mysteriously never makes the brochures). Anyway, it doesn't affect the Fiesta's dynamics overtly. The ride is a bit more gently loping than the regular car's, but it still steers accurately and responsively, and corners as pleasingly as any other car in its class. Dynamically, it's better with the 1.0 petrol engine than the 1.5 diesel - quieter, too - because there's less weight in the nose."

They tried the 138bhp petrol version, which is sprightly, but it can be had for 84bhp; but I reckon you'd want the 98bhp version or higher to make respectable progress (the 0-62mph time falls from 12.7sec to 11.0sec). This 138bhp variant has a claimed 9.4sec 0-62mph time and whizzes along easily. There's appeal to the torque of the 118bhp diesel, but it feels heavier, less agile and transmits a bit of zing into the body.

In 2019 the Active Fiesta's 1.0 litre triple-cylinder won its eleventh 2019 International Engine and Powertrain of the Year (IEPOTY) in the Sub-150 PS category since launch in 2012. The EcoBoost with cylinder deactivation, an industry first, was now used in one Ford in four, more than 1.6 million since 2012 including mild-hybrid Fiesta and Focus. This represented more than 410,000 vehicles from plug-in hybrid Transit Custom van to Tourneo Custom people-mover. Enhancements to the cylinder head, fuel injection and emission-control systems also complemented the core EcoBoost turbocharging, high-pressure direct fuel injection and Twin-independent Variable Cam Timing. Its introduction to further models was planned.

"The 1.0-litre EcoBoost continues to set new benchmarks for compact petrol engines, even seven years and 11 awards after its first International Engine and Powertrain of the Year victory," said Carsten Weber, manager, Research & Advanced Powertrain Engineering, Ford of Europe. "Even with 1.6 million 1.0-litre EcoBoost engines already on the road we're still uncovering its potential. New, even more fuel-efficient electrified powertrains with 1.0-litre EcoBoost at their core are hitting the road soon."

Leather-sated luxury in grown-up Ecosports.

The IEPOTY panel of 70 judges from 31 countries awarded Ford's 1.0-litre EcoBoost a total of 145 points to win the Sub-150 PS category by 26 points, ahead of powertrains from BMW, PSA Group, Toyota/Lexus, and Volkswagen. Following its introduction, the 1.0-litre EcoBoost kick-started an industry trend for small capacity, high output, three-cylinder, turbocharged petrol engines.

"Since winning in 2012, this little jewel has stood the test of time, with most other manufacturers still playing catch-up," said Nicol Louw, Car South Africa and member of the IEPOTY judging panel.

Ford announced that the 1.0 litre EcoBoost engine would provide the basis for the powerful and responsive mild-hybrid powertrains in the new Fiesta EcoBoost Hybrid and Focus EcoBoost Hybrid models, "… further enhancing fuel efficiency while complementing Ford's fun to drive experience. For these sophisticated electrified powertrains, a belt-driven integrated starter/generator (BISG) replaces the standard alternator, enabling recovery and storage of energy usually lost during braking and coasting to charge a 48-volt battery pack."

This BISG also acted as a motor, seamlessly integrating with the engine and using the stored energy to provide torque assistance, which reduced the amount of work required from the petrol engine and helped save fuel. In addition, BISG helped deliver performance, particularly at lower engine speeds for a flexible and connected driving experience. By mitigating turbo-lag it could boost the 1.0 litre up to 155 PS using a larger turbocharger and would be a key ingredient not so much for a lacklustre Ecosport but much more widely towards the Fiesta and Fiesta-replacement family. *Ford*

FIESTA: SALOON: 3-5 door, 4 seats; weight 1.3, 1.4, 1030kg (2270.7lb); 1.6 1040kg (2293lb), TDCi 1060kg (2337lb). Fusion 1070kg (2359lb). 4-cylinders, transverse; 76mm x 76.5mm, 1388cc; cr 11:1; 58kW (77.8bhp) @ 5700rpm; 41.8kW (56.1bhp)/l; 124Nm (91.5lbft) @ 3500rpm. 1.6: 79mm x 81.4mm; 1596cc; 74kW (99.2bhp) @ 6000rpm; 46.4kW (62.2bhp)/l; 146Nm (108lbft) @ 4000rpm. 1.4 TDCi: 73.7mm x 82mm; 1399cc; compr 17.9:1; 50kW (67.1bhp) @ 4000rpm; 35.7kW (47.8bhp)/l; 160Nm (118lbft) @ 2000rpm. 1.6TDCi 75mm x 88.3mm; 1560cc; compr 18:1; 66kW (88.5bhp) @ 4000rpm; 42.3kW (56.7bhp)/l; 204Nm (150.5lbft) @ 1750rpm. 1.3 engine; chain driven single ohc 8-valves; 1.4, 1.6 petrol, 2 belt-driven ohc; 16-valves; aluminium head, block; fuel injection, Siemens engine management; 5-bearing crank. TDCi 1.4, 1 belt-driven ohc; 8-valves, 1.6 2 belt-driven ohc 16-valves; common rail diesels turbocharged. Fwd; hydraulic diaphragm spring sdp clutch; 5-speed synchro manual or Durashift EST; 1.6 opt automatic; final drive 4.06:1, EST 4.25:1, automatic 4.28:1, diesels 3.37:1. Fusion 4.25:1, auto 4.28:1. Steel monocoque; ifs by MacPherson struts, offset coil spring, lower arms on subframe, rear torsion beam axle; tele dampers; anti roll bar; hydraulic vacuum servo split dual circuit disc (Fusion ventilated) and drum brakes, ABS, front discs 25.8cm (10.2in); PAS; 45l (9.9gal) fuel tank; 175/64R14 tyres 5J rims. wheelbase 248.5cm (97.8in); track front 147.5cm (58.1) (Fusion 148cm (58.3in), rear 144.5cm (56.9in); length 391.5cm (154.1in); width 168cm (66.1in); height 146cm (57.5in); ground clearance 14cm (5.51in), Fusion 16cm (6.29in); turning circle 10.3m (33.8ft). Fiesta 4 trim levels: Finesse, Zetec, LX, Ghia airbags, deadlocks, CD player standard. LX electric windows and mirrors, air conditioning. Zetec alloys. Max speed 1.4/16 167kph (104mph); 1.6 183kph (113.9mph); TDCi 1.6 180kph (112.1mph). Fusion 163kph (101.5mph), 178kph (110.9mph), 176mph (282.5kph). 34.5kph (21.49mph), 32.9kph (20.49mph), 42.8kph (26.7mph) @ 1000rpm; 0-100kph (62mph) 13.2sec, 10.6sec, 11.9sec. Fusion 13.7; 10.9, 12.9sec; fuel con 6.6l/100km (42.8mpg), 6.9l/100km (40.6mpg), 4.7l/100km (60.6mpg). Fiesta 1.25 £8495, 1.6 £10,645, 1.4TDCi £9695. Fusion 1.4 £9925, 1.6 £11,525, TDCi £10,695.

Door-hung spare wheel was abandoned.

Fiesta with the windows
blanked off for Fiesta van.

Fast flower seller. Fiesta Sport Van.

FIESTA
VANS

Staples of the telecoms industry, local repairers and small businesses alike, there were Ford vans for every generation. Van versions of Fiestas were popular for all the reasons Fiesta cars were popular. Delivery drivers liked them, they were cheap, economical and practical. Marks I, II, and III had the standard 3-door bodyshell with body-coloured metal instead of the rear side window and a flat floor instead of rear seats. In 1991 the longer-wheelbase Mark III had a high-cube-style and Renault-derived rear torsion bar suspension called The Courier, which continued into the 2002 Mark IV, until it became the Ford Transit Connect. For the Mark V, the standard Fiestavan version was based on the 3-door bodyshell rather than the taller 5-door and a Mark VI Fiesta van was introduced in the European market in 2009.

The one that made its debut at the 2008 IAA Commercial Vehicle Show in Hanover brought practicality, style, and fun to light commercial vehicles. Based on the familiar hatchback it met the needs of professional and personal customers and was available in the UK from Spring 2009. It went on sale from £9,025 to £10,780 with a choice of three engines and three series, entry-level Trend to top-of-the range SportVan. All of them had competitive payloads of 490kg to 515kg, fuel economy up to 67.3mpg and low

insurance groups of 1E and 2E. The addition of the Trend series appealed to a wider group of customers beyond image-conscious businesses. There were many private users who delivered small packages or transported compact equipment such as meter reading tools. Site engineers who did not need a large capacity for tools needed small compact vans. The market was diverse.

Steve Kimber, Ford of Britain's commercial vehicles director, said: "The Fiesta Van is a main player in the car-derived van market, with around 25 per cent of all makes' sales. We expect to build on this, as more and more of today's businesses look to keep their costs under control. The van model was always an integral part of the new Fiesta product plan, and its superior quality really shows. Being competitive has never been more relevant and that's why the Fiesta Van, along with the range-topping SportVan, is a great addition to our 2009 line-up."

Fuel efficiency was claimed to be best in class: the 1.25 litre 82PS Duratec 16V petrol engine had a combined fuel consumption of 49.6mpg and CO2 emissions of 133g/km. There was also a 1.4 litre 68PS Duratorq TDCi turbo diesel, and a 1.6 litre 90PS Duratorq TDCi turbo diesel. According to the newly introduced European Fuel Economy Directive from the EU (EU 80/1268/EEC), both delivered 110g/km CO2 and 4.2l/100

Fiesta vans got EcoBoost hybrid.

km (67.3mpg). The TDCi 90PS had a closed loop coated diesel particulate filter (cDPF) and were both built at the Dagenham plant – also known as Ford's wind-powered plant.

Kimber, also thought, "A commercial vehicle is not just a tool that has to deliver goods in a reliable and cost-efficient way – it's also a business card. The Fiesta van shares many of its key qualities with the car on which it is based. From its driving quality to the latest technologies, this is a practical van for today's image-conscious business world."

The 3-door body shell was a solid foundation. It was safe, agile, and durable and this made it an attractive choice for urban express delivery, service fleets, artisan shops and agreeable to the growing demands of environmental lobbyists.

Like previous Fiesta vans the rear side windows were replaced by body-coloured solid panels, and the rear passenger seats removed to provide space for a step-less load box area. This was about 1,000 litres in volume, with a maximum useable load length of 130cm, and a maximum load box width of 127.8cm (100cm between the wheel arches) and a height of 93.6cm. A half-high bulkhead and solid DIN-compliant tie-down hooks were included.

Using the passenger car as a basis meant it had the same range of technologies and features that gave van drivers an equally safe and enjoyable working environment. The same MacPherson struts in the front and a rear twist-beam suspension provided an equable ride even when loaded and the new EPAS (Electric Power Assisted Steering) system was available as an option to the regular hydraulic. Familiar safety features like ABS anti-lock brakes, including Electronic Brakeforce Distribution (EBD), remained. ESP was also available as an option with all engines as well as Emergency Brake Assist (EBA). Passive safety features included standard front airbags.

Fiesta van drivers had the Ford EasyFuel capless refuelling system that included a mis-fuel inhibitor. This prevented the wrong fuel filler nozzle being inserted, essential for commercial customers with mixed fleets and vehicles used by different drivers.

Other options and accessories included various audio systems such as Bluetooth wireless mobile phone interface, as well as security systems like remote controlled double-locking and a perimeter alarm. All front-wheel-drive Transits could have a 2.2 litre Duratorq TDCi engine of 115PS and 6-speed manual transmission instead of the previous 110PS and 5-speed. The 115PS engine reached peak power at 3,500 rpm, and 15Nm more torque of 300Nm at 1,800-2,000rpm. Standard transmission was the familiar a compact three-shaft Durashift VMT-6.

A 'shorter' gearing in first gear gave an improvement in pulling away from rest, important for delivery drivers on short journeys, and increased towing capacity (up to 5,500kg GTM). The 'longer' gearing in top provided improved highway fuel economy, which could amount to around five per cent with the reduction in engine revs. It also reduced cab noise for more relaxed motorway cruising. Fiesta vans had a

Saloon car facilities for Fiesta van drivers.

Fiesta B-platform grows to Transit size.

resonance. An additional aid to drivers on this and all Transit TDCi models was a gearshift indicator lamp integrated in the tachometer showing optimum moments for gear changes helping economy and engine wear.

From October 2008 all TDCi Transits could be ordered with a closed-loop coated Diesel Particulate Filter (cDPF). The special coating on the filter devices were expected to be maintenance-free, while the closed-loop design and link to the engine management system provided a very high filter efficiency of around 95 per cent.

Fiesta van options included a body colour roof spoiler, electric door mirrors, stereo radio CD, MP3 connection, four front speakers and steering wheel mounted controls. You could have an adjustable steering column, electric windows, while the Trend model had front fog lights, body-coloured, power folding, heated door mirrors, automatic windshield and headlamp wipers, auto dimming rear view mirror, trip computer, driver's seat lumbar support and heated windscreen.

On the SportVan, in addition to Trend features, the 1.6 litre TDCi (90PS) model could have the body -coloured sports "aero" kit, which included high intake front grille, rear bumper and rear spoiler 16in five-spoke sports alloy wheels, Bluetooth hands free and voice control, multi-function display, air conditioning, sports style seats and a leather trimmed steering wheel. A sole trader who wanted to be trendy could specify a rear sports spoiler, perimeter alarm, sports-tuned suspension with lowered ride height and ESP/traction control. The driver's knee and side airbags (head and thorax) and active head restraint were all standard.

Yet, while Fiesta cars remained undisputed best-sellers, especially in the UK, in due course the small van languished, usurped by bigger rivals to the point that by 2018, it very nearly stopped. It suffered firstly in the face of competition from the Ford Transit Courier, also Fiesta-based on the Mark III's longer platform. The Courier also benefitted from belonging to the better-known Transit family. With the Transit identity it was more accomplished, a proper commercial proposition with more space and payload.

So, while the basic small Fiesta van could never shake off being essentially a car without seats, as soon as Ford declared it was going to stop making it and Vauxhall did the same with the Corsa van, Ford changed its mind. Fiesta vans were promptly re-launched in 2018 their only real rivals being the Renault Zoe Van and, of course, still the Courier.

Its return to the commercial vehicle line-up, still based on the current Fiesta passenger car, was accompanied by the inclusion of the game-changing 3-cylinder engine. The Fiesta van was a stylish, compact and economical vehicle for businesses, with a choice of powertrains. The older 1.5 litre Duratorq petrol engine having been dropped, there were now the 1.1 litre 3-cylinder with 85 PS, and 1.0-litre EcoBoost with 125 PS as well as a 1.5-litre TDCi diesel with either 85 PS or 120 PS.

The petrol engines made it effectively a choice between an ordinary Fiesta Van and a Fiesta Sport Van. Nine buyers out of ten

Transit Connect SWB Limited 2.

chose the Fiesta Sport. It had an ST-Line body kit, grippy sports seats and with the excellent turbocharged 3-cylinder EcoBoost Delivery drivers queued up when Ford promised it was, "for customers wanting the ultimate in sporting style for their business, the all-new Fiesta Van is available as a Sport model, with unique front and rear design treatment, colour-coded rocker panels, and up to 18-inch alloy wheels. The sporting theme continues inside the cabin, with revised seats and trim materials, plus unique steering wheel, pedals and gear lever; Adjustable Speed Limiter and Lane Keeping System are fitted as standard."

The 3-door body provided a practical load compartment of around 1.0 cubic metre of cargo space with a load length of almost 1.3 metres and gross payload of 500 kg. The load space had a composite and mesh full bulkhead, durable sidewall trim, and a tough rubber floor covering, with four tie-down hooks. The front compartment was a smart, comfortable working space, trimmed with hard-wearing materials and was profoundly high-tech. Fiesta vans now came with Ford's SYNC 3 communications and entertainment system, compatible with Apple CarPlay and Android Auto. SYNC 3 was optional and had a floating, tablet-inspired 8in colour touchscreen that gave drivers access to key apps from their smartphone using the display for the Waze traffic app and Cisco WebEx. Business customers had the convenience of the FordPass Connect on-board modem for connectivity on the move.

Like the Fiesta passenger car, there was also an unprecedented range of driver assistance technologies to enhance comfort, convenience and safety. These included Ford's Pre Collision Assist with Pedestrian Detection emergency braking system, Adaptive Cruise Control and Blind Spot Information System. Urban van drivers could, according to Ford, "Overcome typical daily challenges, such as Active Park Assist with Perpendicular Parking and Cross Traffic Alert to support easy and safe parking, plus Traffic Sign Recognition and Adjustable Speed Limiter to help avoid speeding fines."

Ford paraded the Fiesta van at the 2018 Birmingham Commercial Vehicle Show with FordPass Connect on-board modem technology enhancing productivity and convenience for businesses. Another innovative solution included Transit Custom plug-in hybrid from the London fleet trial, and a digital service concept for speedy last-mile deliveries. Ford brought connectivity technologies to strengthen its position in the European commercial vehicle market along with a generation of Ford Transit commercial vehicles – including Transit Custom, Transit Connect and Transit Courier models – a return to the urban hatchback van market.

"Connected commercial vehicles will provide exciting new opportunities to create value for our customers, and what we are showing in Birmingham is just the beginning," said Hans Schep, general manager Commercial Vehicles, Ford of Europe. "Supported by our strongest ever vehicle range, Ford is committed to delivering the most efficient solutions to transport goods and people in our cities."

Ford vans served the nation for generations. The 1938 E83W 10cwt served butchers, bakers and candlestick makers.

1951 Fordson 5 cwt was a bargain bereft of tax.

1960s Anglia based Thames van.

1966 Transit van a pop group favourite for the Tremeloes.

Ford had been the top-selling commercial vehicle brand in Europe for three years, consolidating its position 2018 with its best first quarter for Ford commercial vehicle sales since 1993. It displayed one of the plug-in hybrid electric (PHEV) Transit Custom vans currently participating in a 12-month fleet customer trial in London, exploring how hybrid vans could contribute to cleaner air targets in cities.

Live Traffic access was complimentary for the first two years following the purchase of a new Ford featuring SYNC 3 with navigation; thereafter a licence fee was payable. Wi-Fi Hotspot (up to 4G) included complimentary wireless data trial that began at time of activation and expired at the end of three months or when 3GB of data was used, whichever came first. Afterwards a subscription to Vodafone was required.

Ford Transit Connects were top-of-the-range Limited models with alloy wheels, air-conditioning and Bluetooth connectivity as standard. Inside, the load area has been fully ply-lined and specialist roof racks have been fitted to allow external large load carrying. For added security, vehicle tracking devices could be installed. Ford

In 1949 Luigi Chinetti and Lord Selsdon won Le Mans in a 2 litre V12 Ferrari 166MM. Ford was spurred to action.

Ford used motor racing for publicity shots. Jim Clark Jean Shrimpton.

Ford of Britain, Cosworth Engineering and Team Lotus provided Graham Hill with the machinery in 1967.

FIESTAS IN
MOTORSPORT

In the early 1960s Ford Motor Company needed sportier, sexier cars. It had failed key baby boomer buyers with the spectacular flop the Edsel. There was something badly wrong with marketing forecasts. The Car Division's Lee Iacocca decided on a new approach and looked at motor racing. American car manufacturers had long ago agreed not to take part in it. The industry cartel had held fast; motor racing was dangerous, it could be expensive and it was always going to drain engineering resources. The best way to win customers was good old-fashioned advertising.

Now Iacocca, with the blessing of Henry Ford 2, broke with the non-motor-sport treaty, at first only in America, but quickly mounting a challenge in Europe too. Encouraged by Ford in Britain, which was joining forces with Colin Chapman and Lotus, this was a partnership that would take it into Formula 1, Le Mans and win world championships on the road and track all over the world – Ford was going racing.

In America sporty cars meant Italy. Ford was already well into Italian styling with Giacinto Ghia as a design consultant. Ghia had founded a coachbuilding business in 1916, which developed his exclusive Carrozzeria, effectively building up as a car couturier in 1970. Ghia had freshened up VW styling with Karman Ghia Coupes of the 1950s, the Ghia styling studio was proving itself a success. Ford used it as a source and also a Guinea-stamp for Ford models all the way from Escort to Zodiac. Sporty cars and style, to Americans, went together.

To get into Italy's big league Ford wanted to buy an even bigger name. It wanted to buy the biggest and best. It wanted to buy Ferrari. It wanted Ferrari's domination of Le Mans. It wanted to make a Ford-Ferrari and offered $10million. Enzo Ferrari would be free to run his racing team much as he had run Alfa Romeo's as "Scuderia Ferrari" in the 1930s.

It was only a matter of money. Scuderia Ferrari would be identified firmly with Ford.

Unexpectedly, Enzo Ferrari turned it down. Ford was astonished. Henry Ford 2 felt snubbed and obliged to challenge.

America was also fascinated by Le Mans. Think Steve McQueen movies. It was fascinated by Porsches, which were making their way there. Think James Dean, Cholame, California 1955. Le Mans 24-Hours' races saw Cadillacs and specially made sports racers run by millionaire sportsman Briggs Cunningham competing in all post-war. Now Le Mans was opened to manufacturers' prototypes, Ford decided to enter a couple of contenders. It had under development the 1962 Ford Mustang 1, a 1.7-litre, mid-engined open 2-seater designed by Roy Lunn and it was also eyeing up British designer Eric Broadley's Lola GT, a closed coupe. Ford was well advised by shrewd Walter Hayes, Ford of Britain's head of Public Affairs. He would wager £100,000 of Ford money on the DFV Formula 1 engine.

Still, at Le Mans in the 1950s closed coupes were the future. The famous Le Mans start, where the drivers had sprinted across the road to their cars was to provide time for them to put the hood up. Le Mans had been made for touring cars and until the late 1930s that meant open cars. There were still 1960s open 2-seaters like Jaguar C-type and D-types that had had gone down well in America, but now it was sexy closed 2-seaters that were racing down Mulsanne.

The Le Mans plans came together in Ford Advanced Vehicles (FAV), a subsidiary set up

It was 1967 before Ford matched Ferrari. Dan Gurney - AJ Foyt GT40.

in Slough. This drew up a formidable new GT car based on the coupe Lola. A sleek car 40 inches tall, they called it succinctly the GT40. FAV was instructed to win Le Mans with it. Ford supplied its cast iron Fairlane engine and vast resources. Nothing was spared, newly invented computer aided technology was applied. Broadley had only months to produce a competitor and challenge what had taken Ferrari years.

In 1964 the Ford GT40 was tried out at the Le Mans spring test weekend. Two crashed first time out, but by June one, driven by Americans Richie Ginther and Masten Gregory, was ready to race. It took the lead before retiring, but another driven by Phil Hill, who had just fulfilled American dreams by winning the Formula 1 world championship with Ferrari in 1961, set a new lap record at 211.4kph (131.7mph). So much for a quick victory. There seemed more hope in 1965 with GT40 Mark II, but by midnight that effort was in ruins too. All that was achieved was another lap record and the fastest speed on Mulsanne.

Ferrari's hold seemed secure.

Progress took another year, with a 7 litre Galaxie V8 that had scored success in American saloon car racing. Now, the GT40 was big, tough and enormously competent. GT40s competed at the Daytona 24 Hours in February 1966, led almost all the way and took the first three places. At Sebring it won again, came second at Spa, then set new records at Le Mans, finishing first, second and third. Critics complained. It looked like Ford had overwhelmed the opposition, yet Ferrari had around the same number of cars at the start, and all of those with any chance were out by dawn on the second day.

The GT40 graduated to a short series of production cars. By 1967 developments and redesigns were proliferating. They grew

bigger and faster as J-car and Mark IV in various guises. There were two 5.7-litre cars made by John Wyer at Slough and called Mirages, three more GT40s running in Group 2 Sports, making 12 cars in all. Dan Gurney and AJ Foyt not only won Le Mans again at record speed, exceeding 5000km (3107miles) for the first time, but also won the Index of Thermal Efficiency, a distinction highly regarded in France, and usually attained by small fuel-efficient French cars. The Mirages still won outright for the next two years, the first Le Mans ever won by the same car twice, sustaining the competitive life of the design until the end of the decade in the face of determined opposition by Porsche. Ferrari's domination of Le Mans,

which it had won eight times, including an unbroken run from 1960-1965, was over.

1966 GT40 Le Mans winner Mark II works cars specification Coupe; 2-doors, 2-seats; weight 1136.3kg (2505lb), startline 1206.6kg (2660lb). 8-cylinders, 90deg V; mid; 107.5mm x 96.1mm, 6997cc; compr 10.5:1; 361.7kW (485bhp) @ 6200rpm; 69.3bhp (51.7kW)/l; 644Nm (475lbft) @ 5000rpm. Pushrod ohv; aluminium cylinder head, cast iron block; Holley 4-choke carburettor; 5-bearing crankshaft, dry-sump. Rear wheel drive; Long 2 dry plate clutch; 4-speed Ford T-44 synchromesh gearbox in unit with transaxle. Semi-monocoque hull, 23swg sheet steel (.024in) with square tube stiffening, grp body panels reinforced with

Ford Double-Four-Valve (DFV) Cosworth engine.

carbon filament; independent front suspension by double wishbones, coil springs, telescopic dampers, anti roll bar; independent rear suspension by double trailing arms, transverse top link and lower wishbone, coil springs, telescopic dampers, anti-roll bar; hydraulic servo disc brakes, ventilated discs, 29.2cm (11.5in); rack and pinion steering; 159l (35 gal) door sill fuel tanks; cast magnesium wheels, 8.00-15 front, 9.50-15 rear. Wheelbase 241.3cm (95in); track 144.8cm (57in) front, 142.3cm (56in) rear; length 414cm (163in); width 177.8cm (70in); height 102.8cm (40.5in); ground clearance 10cm (3.94in). Cockpit and driver's seat ventilation by air-duct front high-pressure point under nose. Maximum speed timed on Mulsanne 301kph (187.5mph), design estimated 337kph (210mph), still air maximum of early GT40 likely 316.2kph (197mph); 3.1kg/kW (2.3kg/bhp). Production: about 10.

By the late 1970s Ford had not only won Le Mans, it had dominated Formula 1 with the inspired Cosworth DFV in Chapman's Lotuses, winning their first Grand Prix at Zandvoort with Jim Clark who went on to be world champion. Ford Escorts were rally winners, the Cortina a sporting flagship – there was a reputation, up to which all the models in the range had to live.

In 2023 Ford said it would come back to Formula 1 with Red Bull Powertrains, developing a technical partnership for 2026 when the regulations demanded hybrid power units. Bill Ford: "This is the start of a thrilling new chapter in Ford's motorsports story that

Jackie Stewart won championships with Ford engines in his Tyrrell.

Tamed RS for 200 production run.

Radical RS200 raises the dust.

began when my great-grandfather won a race that helped launch our company. Alongside world champions Oracle Red Bull Racing, is returning to the pinnacle of the sport, bringing Ford's long tradition of innovation, sustainability, and electrification to one of the world's most visible stages." Ford and Red Bull Powertrains promised to work to develop the power unit that will be part of the new technical regulations, including a 350kW electric motor and a new combustion engine able to accept sustainable fuels for 2026.

In the 1980s, probably Ford's most radical adventure was a Group B rally car, the RS200. Turbocharged, mid-engined, light, 4-wheel-driven, fast on any surface and transmitting its substantial power down to the road through fat tyres, when it went on sale it was the most expensive Ford to date.

Group B regulations demanded a production run of 200 cars, so Reliant of Tamworth was commissioned to build them. The prototype was announced at Turin in 1984, with production models not reaching the market until 1986. Holding great promise, its rallying career was to be dramatically short however. In the Rally of Portugal, notorious for spectators flooding the special stages, an RS200 went off, killing three. Then in the Tour de Corse, Henri Toivonen and Sergio Cresto died when their Lancia Delta S4 crashed and caught fire. The Fédération Internationale du Sport Automobile (FISA) immediately banned aerodynamic devices on Group B cars and called a halt to the entire class from 1987.

Ford was among the manufacturers that had invested heavily in the category and, faced with the prospect of scrapping the entire production run, converted them from stark rally cars to Ghia luxury specification, trimmed by Tickford and put them on sale. Costly and cramped, noisy and high-revving, the RS200 was physically demanding to drive. It was spectacularly fast with astonishing roadholding and a surprisingly supple ride, yet it was a pure-bred rally car with a GRP 2-seat body on a steel monocoque. The engine went to 7400rpm before rev limiter came in. Gear speeds were 59.4kph (37mph), 102.7kph (64mph), 142.9kph (89mph), and 179.8kph (112mph). Works rally driver Stig Blomqvist gave buyers demo drives at Boreham.

COUPE: 2-doors, 2-seats; weight 1180kg (2601.4lb), rally spec 1050kg (2315lb). 4-cylinder mid; 86mm x 77.62mm, 1803cc; cr 8.2:1; 184kW (246.7bhp) @ 6500rpm; 102.1kW (136.8bhp)/l; 292Nm (215lbft) @ 4500rpm. Rally versions 283kW (380bhp), track versions 485kW (650bhp). BDT (Belt Drive camshafts Turbocharged) inclined 23deg right; 2 belt-driven overhead cams; 4-valves; aluminium cylinder head, block; Bosch fuel injection, EEC-IV engine management; 5-bearing crankshaft; Garrett T03/04 turbocharger .8bar (11.6psi), rally version 1.2bar (17.4psi). Four wheel drive with optional rear-drive only; torque split 37% front 63% rear; lockable centre differential splits 50/50; 5-speed all-indirect gearbox at front separate from engine; diaphragm spring twin plate AP 18.4cm (7.25in) clutch; helical spur primary drive; final drive epicyclic Ferguson with viscous coupling limited slip, 4.375:1. Stressed platform; floor and bulkheads Ciba-Geigy honeycomb sandwich; steel front and rear extensions; bolt-on tubular stiffening subframes link suspension towers to central structure; ifs and irs by double wishbones with twin coil spring damper units and anti-roll bars, adjustable at front; adjustable toe-in control link at rear, alternative ride heights, adjustable spring platform positions; hydraulic servo brakes, 28.5cm (11in) ventilated discs, dual circuit; rack and pinion; 2 tanks 73.6l (16.2 gal) & 41.8l (9.2 gal) total 115.4l (25.4 gal); Pirelli P700 225/50VR16 tyres, 8in rims, Speedline 3-piece composite alloys. Wheelbase 253cm (99.6in); track 150cm (59.1in) front, 149.7cm (58.9in) rear; length 400cm (157.5in); width 176.5cm (69.5in); height varies about 132cm (52in); ground clearance varies about 18cm (7.1in); turning circle 9.6m (31.5ft). Road car had insulated cover to sound-damp engine, grey carpet, cloth seats, leather-rimmed steering wheel, no radio. Maximum speed 225kph (140.2mph); 32.4kph (20.2mph) @ 1000rpm; 0-100kph (62mph) 6.1sec Autocar; 6.4kg/kW (4.8kg/bhp); fuel consumption 17l/100km (16.6mpg). £45,000. production 200.

The Fiesta as a rally car was lower-key and never attained the heights of the Escorts. There were two hopefuls in the 1979 Monte

Carlo Rally, one driven by Roger Clark and Jim Porter, and a German entry with Ari Vatanen and David Richards. They had been highly modified with motorsport components including limited-slip differentials. Engines were competition-prepared 1,600 cc Kent crossflows, which also appeared in the Mark 1 Fiesta XR2. They did well in the ice and snow and while Clark failed to make his mark, the German car finished ninth, providing encouragement for the launch of Fiesta XR2.

Yet, while Fiesta marketing had its sports editions including Supersport, XR2, S(Sport), XR2i, Si, RS Turbo, RS1800, Zetec S, Zetec RS, and ST with a range of engines from the Kent to the Duratec, the competitions department kept the model mostly in reserve.

The rationale of Ford production engineering was to use as many components, as many times as possible, which sometimes had unexpected results. Introduced to improve the Mark II Cortina's performance by widening the spread of its pulling power, the Kent engine of 1967 was a free-revving and almost unburstable unit, that not only became the basis of Ford's mainstream production cars but was also a resounding success in motor sport. It was used for the Formula Ford single seaters and its crankcase and crankshaft were the building blocks for the BDA Ford Cosworths, giving 85.8kW (115bhp) in road tune and anything up to 212.5kW (285bhp) @ 9000rpm for racing.

It went on to become one of the best and for 16 years, besides several marks of Cortina, saw service in Fiestas, Escorts, and Capris with its basis a singularly robust 5-bearing crankshaft and a new crossflow cylinder head with inlet ports on one side, exhausts on the other. The 1.3-cylinder head

1999 World Rally Championship Fiesta-related Focus.

Chrono Fiesta WRC at 2010 Paris Show.

M-sport Fiesta.

own control blade system, and increased suspension travel to 20cm for gravel stages.

It wouldn't be until 2002 before a RallyeConcept Fiesta materialised following collaboration between Ford RallyeSport, the motorsport experts behind the Puma Super 1600, and the Focus World Rally Championship competitors. Ford Design Europe was the creative team behind the 3-door Fiesta on which it was based.

A development programme was brought in to meet Fédération Internationale de l'Automobile (FIA) homologation by the middle of 2003, which Ford RallyeSport expected to be a success. It made its debut at Rally Greece 2004 with a Fiesta Super 1600.

In March 2006 a Fiesta Sporting Trophy was a one-make championship based around the Fiesta ST Group N with 165 PS 121 kW (163 bhp) 2-litre Duratec ST engines, with M-Sport conversion kits that provided the safety equipment and performance upgrades enabling it to be competitive and reliable. A year later the Pirtek Rally Team introduced the Fiesta Super 2000 to compete in the Australian Rally Championship.

The 2009 the Mark VI Fiesta S2000, although not due for homologation until the following year and built to compete in the WRC, got an unofficial launch as course car on the final round of the International Rally Championship Rally Scotland. In 2013 M-Sport developed the Fiesta R5, successor of the S2000, based on the 1.6 litre Fiesta ST. This was designed for Group 5.

With new WRC regulations M-Sport developed the Fiesta RS WRC, based on Fiesta S2000. It won six WRC rounds in 2011 and 2012, driven by Jari-Matti Latvala, Mikko Hirvonen and Mads Ostberg. However, since M-Sport lost most of its manufacturer support for 2013 it wasn't able to win. In 2013, Thierry Neuville was the world championship runner-up, being a M-Sport junior works driver. Fiesta RS WRC has been popular among private drivers, due to its good driveability, reasonable price and availability.

was completely flat and the 1.6 had only small recesses, since the combustion chambers were entirely contained within the pistons.

The Fiesta-related Focus was a winner almost from the start in the World Rally Championship (WRC). Colin McRae finished third in the 1999 Monte Carlo Rally, only to be excluded on a technicality. An oversized water pump resulted in a 2-week development programme at the Ford competitions department in Boreham, reputedly costing £500,000 to make certain a standard one would work just as well. The turbocharged and intercooled engine was a close relative of the production Focus. It used a standard iron block, conformed strictly with the design criteria as rebuilt by Mountune

It used design tolerances and electronics to eliminate turbo lag and the drive was taken by a bevel gear from the tilted transverse engine to a longitudinal 6-speed gearbox.

The drive went to all four wheels by way of a central differential that split the torque 50:50, then to two more diffs front and rear. The front and central diffs had hydraulic locks controlled by microprocessor programs to deal with the broadside cornering required by loose-surface high speed driving. A regulation safety roll cage gave immense strength to a body shell that looked every inch a Focus, keeping many of the standard car's features, if not precisely at least in spirit. It had MacPherson struts front and rear, where it replaced the Focus's

SALOON: 3-doors, 2-seats; weight 1230kg (2711.7lb). 4-cylinders; front; transverse, 1989cc; 223.7kW (300bhp) @ 6000rpm; 112.5kW (150.8bhp)/l; 551Nm (406lbft) @ 4000rpm. 2 belt-driven ohc; 4-valves; aluminium cylinder head, iron block; Garrett turbocharger, electronic engine management; 5-bearing crankshaft. Four-wheel drive; M-Sport X-Trac 240; 6-speed sequential; final drive to choice; electronic control of locking differentials. Steel monocoque supported by roll cage; reinforced chassis rails; ifs by MacPherson struts and adjustable links; adjustable telescopic dampers; hydraulic servo 30cm (11.8in) ventilated disc brakes; ABS; rack and pinion PAS; 120l (26.4 gal) tank; 7Jx15in wheels, choice of tyres. Wheelbase 263.5cm (103.7in); length 415.2cm (163.5in); width 177cm (69.7in); height 142cm (55.9in). Sparco seats, safety harness, intercom, calculating and navigation equipment. Maximum speed approx 225kph (140mph); 0-100kph (62mph) 4.3sec, 0-160kph (100mph) 10.0sec; 5.5kg/kW (4.1kg/bhp).

Fiesta RS WRC.

**Nearly 35 years from
Fiesta 1 Fiesta VII.**

2008 FIESTA VII:
FIESTA FINALE

By the first decade of the 21st century it looked as though Ford had attained its global automotive Holy Grail. World-wide single designs had been languishing. Ford managed it with the Model T. A hundred years later it was mastering the practicalities of making technical specifications of core models to be the same everywhere so that the precious volume statistics for major components held up. Common causes world-wide helped. A world class Fiesta on a Mazda had been tempting. Fiesta IV and Mazda 121 shared most features, used the same components, and could be built on the same assembly lines. The Mazda gained a good reputation for reliability through endorsement by the well-recognised JD Power reliability surveys, although sold fewer.

Ford and Mazda of Japan had started a partnership in 1974 and by 1979 Ford had a 24.5 per cent stake, by 1995 33.4 per cent and there were common models such as the B-series pick-up truck and several joint developments. If a car's fundamentals could be made suitable for Europe and Asia, and they demonstrably did, North America, Nanjing China, Australia and South Africa would easily follow.

By the time of Fiesta VII however, the 2008 financial crisis was taking effect. Ford reduced its stake in Mazda. Plans nurtured since Ford's Premier Automotive Group was founded in 1999 were being dismantled. Lincoln deleted in 2002; its LS had shared platform and engines with Jaguar S-types and Aston Martin was sold in 2007 for £479million. Land Rover, which had been acquired from BMW in 2000 after the collapse of the old Rover Group was sold, along with Jaguar to Tata in March 2008 for £1.15billion. By 2010 Volvo went off to Geely of China for £1.8 billion.

It was just as well the Fiesta went on, constant, almost unchanging, gaining the influential *What Car?* magazine's car of the year title in 2009. A World Rally Championship Fiesta RS was previewed at the Paris Motor Show in 2010 and promptly made a clean sweep of the Swedish Rally podium in 2011.

Special Editions remained a marketing tool, beginning with the Mark 1's Sandpiper until

June 2008's Fiesta ST500. This special edition had Panther black metallic paint, black alloy wheels red brake callipers - a first for any Fiesta - silver bonnet and side stripes. Prices started at £15,000, with extra equipment and limited to just 500. Starting with a 2.0 litre 150PS engine, sports-tuned steering, lowered and stiffened sports suspension and a short-shift, close ratio gearbox, Ford's sporting heritage was emphasised with unique 'U'-shaped stripes that echoed the livery of the Escort RS2000. The Fiesta ST500 also had carbon fibre pattern interior trim, a Sony audio system and ebony leather heated seats.

There was also a new sporty Fiesta Zetec S. Red special edition which came in Colorado red paint, with black and white chequered flag roof, leather seats and privacy glass cost £13,000. There were only 400 of those made, following the success of the popular radian yellow "Anniversary" and lime green "Celebration" models which sold out within weeks in response to enthusiastic dealership occasions. The Ford Fiesta had been in the top three best-selling vehicles in Britain every month with 42,895 models being sold up to the end of May 2008, almost 20 per cent of the British small car market.

Specials with picturesque names also included limited-edition Ford Fiesta Titanium Individuals, with six series and five engine options. Studio, Edge, ECOnetic, Zetec, Titanium and Zetec S models with 1.25 petrol and choices of 1.4-litre petrol or diesel or 1.6 petrol or diesel engines. Studio had electric

front windows as standard, Edge had air conditioning and at the sporty end the Zetec S series with alloy pedals, sporty side skirts a Quickclear windscreen become standard.

There was more to marketing than power and speed however. The 2008 London Motor Show the Fiesta Zetec S was also available with a 1.6-litre 90PS Duratorq TDCi diesel, providing a more relaxed driving character. The flexible engine gave 67.3mpg, generated just 110g/km CO2, yet it developed a towering 204 Nm torque pulling power from a modest slow revving 1,750 rpm. It had a commendable mid-range performance.

Pressure was still growing for engine efficiency and a frugal Fiesta at the motor show completed the company's small, medium and large car ECOnetic line-up. This was a 76.3mpg Ford Fiesta ECOnetic. Claimed as Britain's greenest family car with CO2 emissions of 98g/km, it went on sale from £11,800 at the end of the year, joining the existing Mondeo and Focus ECOnetic, which led a 38 per cent sales increase in the first half of the year in sub-120g/km CO2 vehicles powered by Dagenham's 1.4/1.6 TDCi engines. Earlier a sub-140g/km Ford Mondeo ECOnetic went on sale with official figures for the 1.6 TDCi Urban 61.4mpg, Extra Urban 88.3mpg making a combined 76.3mpg.

The Fiesta ECOnetic was spreading more straws in the wind. Driver aids were proliferating. Lane-change detection, radar detection of vehicle distances in cruise controls were commonplace. Its green shift indicator in the instrument cluster highlighting the optimal point to change gear for best fuel economy was another innovation maintained for the Fiesta's eventual successor. Its claims to be the most fuel efficient 5-seat family car with CO2 emissions under 100g/km made it zero rated both for Vehicle Excise Duty (VED) or road tax and for the showroom tax element of VED introduced for the first year of ownership in the 2008 Budget.

Aerodynamic shaping, lowered suspension, low resistance 175/65R14 tyres and low friction oil helped it achieve such low CO2 emissions. Roelant de Waard, Ford of Britain chairman and managing director, said: "Many drivers are prepared to be green – but still want comfort, performance and an affordable price. ECOnetic answers that demand." Fiesta product manager, Chris Muers: "Typically, around 10 per cent of small car buyers specify an auto option, so convenience technology is an important addition to a range that now offers an option for every taste and need," as the 1.4-litre automatic went on sale now from £13,195 on-the-road from June 2009.

Durashift's hydraulically controlled system of clutches was managed by its own electronic control system called Transmission Control Module (TCM), which read the amount of pressure applied to the fly-by-wire throttle and adjusted the gear changes. It all depended on style, which meant that with enthusiastic driving the gearbox changed later and faster but did it slower if only small amounts of throttle were used. Moving the lever to the right gave a Tiptronic-style manual selector.

Autocar testers, however, were unimpressed. It applauded the auto Fiesta well enough in three different levels of trim: Style Plus, Zetec and Titanium, trying Style+ with heated windscreen and air-conditioning. But Durashift only came in 95bhp 1.4-litre petrol engine variants, and apart from what *Autocar* described as a "questionable" blue dashboard, "...considering the car's futuristic interior the auto lever itself looks perhaps a tiny bit dated, or at least a little sober in this environment. The Fiesta rides well for a small car and is immediately comfortable thanks to a good driving position, so the thought of letting the gearbox do the work automatically is not unappealing. Unfortunately, after a few miles what should be a relaxing experience becomes the opposite. The 4-speed auto changes smoothly but seems far too eager to drop a cog at the faintest whiff of throttle. Sneeze and it will change down two gears. Hold the throttle down without kickdown and intriguingly it will hold the car to, and on, the rev limiter. Often the 'box will change down into a gear leaving the engine spinning at a noisy 5500rpm. This seems to be against the nature of having an automatic, and especially against the nature of the market for an automatic Fiesta."

They were also disappointed by the performance, and sorry the gearbox did not have a "sport" setting since 0-60mph occupied a leisurely 13.9sec. The newer lighter body was some 40kg lighter than before, which meant the auto-equipped car delivered a commendable 43.4mpg and a CO_2 of 154g/km although the Fiesta's exemplary chassis set-up still struck a good balance between lively handling and a pliant ride, a testament to careful initial good proportions set by 1970's designers and many years of careful development.

"Often with automatics that have manual modes it is best to leave them in 'D', but this is often not the case with the Fiesta. It doesn't change particularly quickly but on many roads progress will be smoother when you are doing the work yourself. If you want a Fiesta and an auto 'box then this is the only one. However, the car would work better with more power and a less change-happy nature so perhaps it would be worth considering the 7-speed VW Polo 1.4."

Yet by the 2009 Frankfurt Motor Show Ford was looking further ahead. Turbocharging had been well established for enhancing the power output of high-performance cars but it was less apparent that it might have a far wider future. Turbochargers, or turbosuperchargers as they used to be called, had increased the urge of aero engines flying ever higher in the 1940s; Making them smaller allowed them to be put into cars in the 1980s. By the 21st century they were miniaturised enough to make them a key to open doors hitherto undreamt-of.

A highly developed new generation of tiny turbos using light new materials and constructed with watch-making precision that allowed them to spin at unimaginable speeds was known as EcoBoost with Ford's imaginative lexicon of novel titles. They almost led to a replay of the 20th century

Ford relinquished Premier Automotive conquests. Aston Martin V8 Vantage Roadster.

initiative of lean-burn combustion Ford bravely pioneered but which foundered on the wholesale adoption of catalytic converters by short-termist legislators. The new EcoBoost high-efficiency low-CO_2 4-cylinder petrol engines announced in the sprawling halls of the Frankfurt Motor Show still some way ahead of their production applications. It would be fully a year before they saw the light of a production day and the best part of a decade before they made their full impact. They had direct injection, turbocharging, twin independent variable valve timing to maximise combustion efficiency and their fuel consumption and CO_2 emissions promised reductions of 20 per cent compared to conventional engines of similar power.

"The new family of Ford EcoBoost four-cylinder petrol engines coming in 2010 is a key element of Ford Motor Company's global blueprint for sustainability," said John Fleming, Chairman & CEO, Ford of Europe. "We believe they will provide a genuinely attractive alternative to diesel or hybrid power units, delivering highly competitive fuel economy and cost-of-ownership, along with the responsive performance and wide rev range, which have made petrol engines the favoured choice for so many."

Titanium Fiesta 2009.

Fiesta Titanium sophistication.

Fragmented Fiesta made more room for people.

2008 engine.

The initial 4-cylinder range was only the start. EcoBoost made downsizing, putting the performance of a large capacity engine with the fuel economy of something much smaller within reach. For future Fiestas and their ultimate replacements, they were extremely significant. Here was miniaturisation of a sort that had reduced powerful computers from room-sized to hand-held, an engine family that focussed on two 4-cylinder units of 1.6 litre and 2.0 litre capacities and held the promise of an even more advanced small-capacity unit later.

For 2010 the line-up comprised engines for the C-MAX and larger cars. They expanded the range of applications with small and medium cars. Ford confirmed that its 2.0 litre EcoBoost engine would go global, launching in North America in 2010 and, for its first rear-wheel drive application, also in the Ford Falcon in Australia from 2011. "With the 2.0-litre engine catering for applications of 200PS and above, the 1.6 litre engine spanning the 150-180PS range, and the small-capacity unit meeting the demand for engines in the sub-130PS segment, over time we will offer a high-efficiency low-CO2 Ford EcoBoost engine for all of our major European vehicle lines," said Fleming.

There were three critical elements. Powertrain engineers exploited the economy and emissions improvements, creating a new combustion system combining the benefits of high-pressure direct fuel injection, advanced high-speed turbocharging, and twin independent variable valve timing. Each had advantages of their own, all three together brought significantly enhanced performance through a more efficient combustion process across a full operating range.

EcoBoost had many of the benefits offered by the best compression-ignition diesels without losing the driving character and cost advantages of a petrol engine. Strong low speed pull and responsive performance across the full rev range survived, importantly with an affordable practical way to reduce carbon emissions.

With echoes of the old lean-burn initiative, this was a combustion system that ignited fuel efficiently and cleanly. At its heart was a high-pressure direct injection system which injected each cylinder with small, precise sprays at a pressure of up to 200 bar. The droplet size was typically smaller than 0.02mm, one-fifth the width of human hair. Direct injection produced a cooler, denser charge. As in modern diesels, multiple injections were also possible per combustion cycle, further enhancing economy and emissions.

Variable valve timing on both intake and exhaust camshafts helped the 4-cylinder engines optimise gas flow at all speeds, improving things particularly at part load, delivering the same strong low-end torque that had always made diesels so popular. The refined and responsive performance across the full range was made possible by the new small, low inertia turbo rotors spinning at more than 200,000rpm. These achieved maximum torque at 1,500rpm or lower almost immediately. Turbo engines had always suffered from a time lag; drivers wanted quick acceleration in traffic. EcoBoost supplied it.

The change was also largely brought about by charge-cooling the direct injection at low engine speeds. Variable valve timing helped through a scavenging effect that increased air flow through the engine and boosted low-speed torque. This careful matching of the turbo ensured EcoBoost engines were powerful and responsive at more than 5,000rpm while providing the wide spread of power of a typical diesel.

EcoBoost thus provided a smaller capacity engine that could replace larger naturally aspirated ones. Turbocharging typically gave 50 per cent more torque, so here was a significant opportunity to downsize engines while providing the same performance. Efficiency was also improved through reduced internal friction, lower pumping losses, and lighter weight. Little engines warmed up faster helping real-world economy.

The 1.6- and 2.0-litre Ford EcoBoost units were advanced lightweight 4-cylinder families. Both were aluminium, with 16-valve DOHC cylinder heads and twin independent variable cam timing. Refined with optimised lubrication system design and low-friction coatings, met stringent global emissions requirements including the PZEV (partial zero emission vehicles) standard in California as well as European Stage V.

Production was widespread. The 2.0 litre was produced at Valencia, while the 1.6 was made at Bridgend. Ford was able to say that a future advanced small-displacement EcoBoost was planned for both Cologne and the new Craiova Engine Plant in Romania. This east European facility was becoming a cornerstone of the near-term sustainability plan, not only for Fiesta, but also its long-term replacement the Puma still years ahead.

Romania had been one of the biggest car makers in eastern Europe during its years in the communist bloc. It had mostly collapsed in the aftermath of the 1989 revolution, although German and far-east companies were keen to open it up again. Ford paid $57 million and promised to invest $923 million in a former Daewoo factory in the south-west of the country, to start making Transit Connect and B-Max. Within seven years, the Romanian motor industry would be back to the fifth biggest in central and eastern Europe behind the Czech Republic, Slovakia, and Poland.

Ford Europe president John Fleming and Calin Popescu-Tariceanu, Prime Minister of Romania, chose the 2007 Frankfurt Motor Show to begin the process of transferring ownership of the facility. Fleming: "This is great news for Ford, for Romania and for Craiova. We are acquiring a plant with a skilled and enthusiastic workforce and together we will work to transform the plant into an industry benchmark for vehicle manufacturing in central Europe." Prime Minister Tariceanu: "Ford has shared with us their exciting vision for the future of Craiova. In time the plant will be producing over 300,000 Ford vehicles and engines a year, all proudly made in Romania."

Ford was planning to make 1.3 million EcoBoost engines a year. Some 750,000 of them would be for the United States, where turbo diesels for cars was less common. In North America EcoBoost was to be the first gasoline, direct-injection, twin-turbocharged engine ever manufactured. The technology was being used for a 3.5 litre EcoBoost V6,

Romanian pact secured.

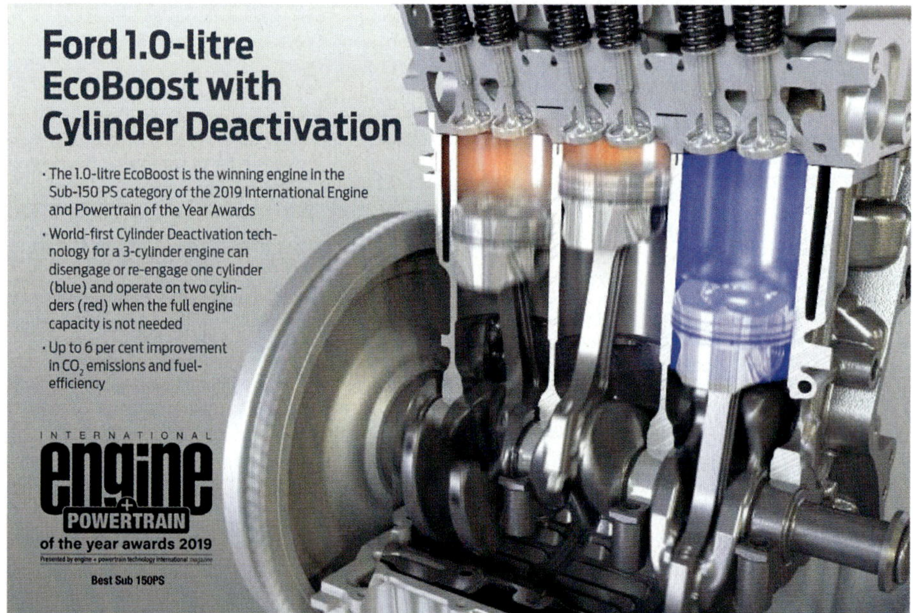

Breakthrough. One litre, three cylinder, EcoBoost.

Engine of the year fits in a car.

More demand for MPG.

Autocar's Steve Cropley supervises MPG Marathon.

MPG Marathon winners.

offering similar power but better fuel economy than V8 competitors in the Ford Taurus SHO with 370PS. It was also in the 2010 Ford Flex, Lincoln MKS and MKT with 360PS and a responsive 475 Nm of torque. By 2013 Ford expected to put EcoBoost engines in 90 per cent of its global products.

The new design set the stage not only for the Mark VIII Fiesta, but also its successor. By the second decade of the 21st century one Fiesta was being sold every two minutes, but the strongest straw in the wind of change came in 2012 with the 3-cylinder engine. Introduced first in Focus, this 1.0 litre combined turbocharging, direct fuel injection and twin variable valve timing, along with the same novel integrated exhaust manifold. The 3-cylinder had an offset crank and variable oil pump, dual-split cooling system, an unbalanced flywheel pulley and was promised for B-Max and C-Max models within the year.

The innovations made it a more strenuous alternative to bigger engines with 125PS and 170Nm peak torque (200Nm with overboost) between 1,400 and 4,500rpm, as well as fuel economy improvements over the outgoing 1.6 litre 125PS of the 5-door Focus. Most importantly, it was astonishingly compact. It took up no more room on the car floorplan than a sheet of foolscap paper.

Three-cylinder engines had been tried before, notably some brave field trials with a 2-stroke Fiesta back in 1989. Now Thomas Zenner, Ford powertrain engineering supervisor assured: "With this engine there is no compromise: it delivers best-in-class fuel economy, outstanding driveability and excellent refinement – achieved by combining advanced features with smart engineering."

Like the other EcoBoosts, the key ingredient of the triple-cylinder was its small low-inertia turbocharger. Its lightweight turbo blades spinning quickly up to speed in the exhaust flow, reduced the lag in response during acceleration. This turbo's catch-up time was almost imperceptible. Variable timing on both intake and exhaust camshafts gave power range flexibility and a water-cooled exhaust manifold integrated into the cylinder head lowered exhaust temperature. There was optimal fuel-to-air ratio even at high speeds, for real-world fuel economy, while the offset crank and variable oil pump ensured the engine kept an optimum oil pressure throughout the speed range. High pressure solenoid direct injectors provided a cooler and denser fuel-to-air ratio, and the dual-split cooling system had two thermostats for quicker engine warm up.

The cambelt ran in oil to reduce friction and the unbalanced flywheel pulley addressed the noise and vibrations inherent in a 3-cylinder. Odd numbers produced imbalance, leading to pitch and yaw stresses and booming noises. Instead of a conventional balancer shaft to counteract this, the flywheel and crank pulley were intentionally "unbalanced" to offset the primary engine shaking forces.

The 3-cylinder soon won prizes. Launched first in the European Focus, it was named 2012 "International Engine of the Year", the "Best New Engine" and the "Best Engine Under 1.0-litre" in awards presented by *Engine Technology International* magazine. Voted on by 76 journalists from 35 countries, it coincided with Dagenham celebrating making its 40 millionth engine of all sorts since 1931.

The International Engine of the Year Award had been going since 1998 and this was the first time Ford had won it. With 28 per cent more points than its closest rival, as well as the highest points total of any engine in the competition's history, Joe Bakaj, Ford global powertrain vice president, was understandably delighted: "We set the bar incredibly high when we started to design this engine. We wanted to deliver eye-popping economy, surprising performance, quietness, and refinement from a very small, 3-cylinder engine. The team responded to this challenge with some exciting innovation. The result is a game-changer for petrol engines globally."

He was right. Chairman of the International Engine of the Year awards, editor of *Engine Technology International* magazine, said: "This is a fitting victory for a truly remarkable engine. For a 3-cylinder to power a vehicle like the Ford Focus with such ease proves that the future is very bright for the internal combustion engine."

Judges praised: "If downsizing is the way ahead, there is currently no better example than this. Same power as the naturally aspirated 1.6-litre engine it replaces, and much punchier to drive. With good torque at the very low end, this high-tech 3-cylinder turbo gives the driving performance of a small turbo diesel, but without noise and vibrations." Christophe Congrega of France's *L'Automobile* Magazine.

It also notched up a major with the Dewar Trophy for 2012. Presented for outstanding British technical achievement in the automotive industry since 1906 when it went to the 127.6mph Stanley steam car; 1907 to Rolls-Royce and in 1908 to Cadillac for pioneering parts interchangeability. The Royal Automobile Club now presented it to Graham Hoare,

Ford team whimsy fits lights and mudguards.

Head of the Ford Dunton Technical Centre, and members of the EcoBoost engineering team.

"Ford's engineers at Dunton have produced an outstanding downsized powertrain that delivers exceptional economy while achieving the high torque and relaxed driving characteristics normally associated with a diesel and the smooth, free-revving qualities of a petrol engine, that has won acclaim from everyone who has driven it," said John Wood MBE, Chairman of the Dewar Technical Committee.

Steve Cropley, Dewar Technical Committee member and Editor-in-Chief of *Autocar* added: "Ford's 1.0-litre EcoBoost engine sets extraordinary new standards of efficiency, refinement and driver appeal — and brings them to the mass of British drivers who buy and drive affordable cars."

The tiny engine soon showed its paces on a track. A Formula Ford racing car produced a convincing performance at the Nürburgring in September 2012, recording the 11th fastest lap ever at the Nordschleife circuit in 7 min 22 sec (better than some 600 horsepower supercars) with a top speed of 255.5 km/h (158.8 mph) and a 0-100 km/h (0-62 mph) time of less than four seconds. The vehicle completed the 20.832 km (12.94 mile) Nordschleife at an average of 169 km/h (105 mph) after Ford patiently took months changing the customary regulation 180 PS, 1.6-litre EcoBoost power unit with a specially tuned 205 PS version of the 3-cylinder. The project team even made the single-seater street legal, with wheel covers, front and rear lights and indicators, aerodynamic wing mirrors and a horn. It had a 6-speed manual gearbox and road-legal tyres.

Go-Faster Stripes returned in 2010. S1600.

Cologne production line greets 2017 Fiesta.

Britain imported its Fiestas.

Outdoorsy Fiesta Active quasi SUV.

"We wanted to prove that size doesn't matter by showing everyone what an amazingly capable engine we have developed in the 1.0-litre EcoBoost," said Roelant de Waard, vice president of Marketing and Sales, Ford of Europe. "What better way than by beating some of the best supercars in the world on the Nordschleife, while using a fraction of the fuel." In-house tests suggested the 1.0-litre EcoBoost-powered Formula Ford was extremely frugal, delivering 2.4 l/100 km (118 mpg) at 56 km/h (35 mph), and 5 l/100 km (57 mpg) at 120 km/h (75 mph).

In 2013 a new 182 PS Fiesta ST took nearly 10,000 orders in Europe in its first six months. Twice as many as expected. The following year the Fiesta red edition and Fiesta black edition, fitted with the 140PS 1.0 Ecoboost, was the most powerful 1.0 litre production engine ever. It had more power per-litre than a Bugatti Veyron. By the time of the 25,000th Fiesta in 2017, the awards were continuing. It was named *Carbuyer's* Car of the Year, *Top Gear* magazine's Best Supermini, Best Budget Car at Women's World Car of the Year and Best Used Small Car by *What Car?* magazine, which also made it Best Small Car in its Used Car of the Year Awards.

Editor Stuart Milne said: "It is Britain's favourite car year in, year out, and the latest is the best yet. It looks great inside and out. Buyers can choose from tremendous audio upgrades, autonomous driving features and levels of luxury in the top-spec Vignale, - unthinkable a few years ago." Fiesta engineer Robert Stiller, who collected the Carbuyer award, said: "After 8 years as UK best seller, expectations were high for the new Fiesta. To win Carbuyer Car of the Year half-way through its launch is an accolade for the whole Fiesta product development team. We have further models coming next year in the rugged Active and hot ST models – hopefully UK car buyers will love those just as much."

The Women's World Car of the Year panel had 25 female car experts from 20 countries, picked the Fiesta from 10 finalists. Panellist Sandy Myrhe: "Fiesta was such a consistent nomination among our judges that it scored highly in our Supreme category too, with more votes than high-end models including Aston Martin and the Range Rover Velar."

Ford also scored twice at Scottish Car of the Year (SCOTY) in 2017, with the Focus RS Mountune, named as Hot Hatch of the Year and the Fiesta Best Supermini. Of the 4.5 million British Fiesta sales since 1976, half a million had been in the territory of The Association of Scottish Motoring Writers.

In 2017 production in Cologne followed a €293 million investment. A Fiesta was coming off the line every 68 seconds. For a sixth year the 1.0 litre EcoBoost was Best Engine Under 1.0-litre in the International Engine of the Year, its tenth award since 2012. Fiestas were withdrawn from the Americas, Australasia and Asia replaced, said Ford, by SUVs and pickups like the Ranger and Escape.

Fiesta EcoBoosts of 2019 with 48-volt mild hybrid technology, coincided with the launch of the ultimate Fiesta replacement, the Puma compact crossover, Ford cheerfully admitting it was created from Fiesta architecture. In 2020 novelties introduced to Fiesta included

Adaptive Cruise Control with Stop & Go, FordPass with remote vehicle features, and what Ford called Perpendicular Park Assist. There was a Fiesta ST Edition with unique Azura Blue exterior, adjustable coilover suspension and flow-formed alloy wheels, limited to 500 in Europe.

By 2021 that was effectively the final Fiesta. There were new exteriors and Vignale pack variants, Matrix LED headlamps with glare-free high beam, 12.3in customisable instrument display and among, "… a suite of sophisticated driver assistance technologies" a Wrong-Way Alert. Yet more important was an electrified powertrain line-up that had a 48-volt EcoBoost Hybrid and a 7-speed Powershift dual-clutch. Fiesta was still sharing technology with its successor but it was now at last, "future-ready" to bow out and prepare to hand over to the Puma, which was already well into production in Romania and selling alongside it.

The Fiesta's Wrong-Way alert's windscreen-mounted camera co-ordinated information from the sat-nav to provide audible and visual warning should drivers go through two "No Entry" signs, such as on a motorway approach ramp. It also read speed limit signs and flashed them on to the instrument panel, a boon to drivers anxiously keeping within the law. There was a plethora of other driver-assistance technology. The Adaptive Cruise Control with Stop & Go and Speed Sign Recognition, helped maintain distance from vehicles ahead, and cars fitted with Powershift transmission could be brought to a halt and then pulled away again in stop-start traffic.

"Active Park Assist" detected Fiesta-sized spaces and could control the steering to

Smoothing out the lines. 2008.

park hands-free nose-to-tail and side-by-side. While acceleration, braking and gear selection were left to the driver, buyers of Mark I Fiestas in 1975 would have been astonished with all the mechanisms designed to prevent or mitigate the effect of collisions, such as "Blind Spot Information System (BLIS) with Cross Traffic Alert and Active Braking, Lane-Keeping Aid and Pre-Collision Assist with Active Braking" – Ford PR was fond of capitals.

Those early customers might have been suspicious of the advanced connectivity features that Ford thought helped, "…enjoy stress-free ownership experiences." Standard FordPass Connect modem technology allowed convenient features to be selected remotely using an app to operate "Door Lock/Unlock, Remote Start, Vehicle Locator and Vehicle Status" to check fuel level, make sure the alarm was set, tyre pressures, oil life and more. "Live Traffic" updated the sat-nav and

Regenerations 1993 XR2i shares the track with 2011 Fiesta.

2018 Final Fiestas.

enabled "Local Hazard Information" to tell drivers of dangers ahead - even an accident round the next corner.

SYNC 3 gave control of audio, navigation and connected smartphones by voice commands through "Apple CarPlay and Android Auto" through an 8in central touchscreen with pinch and swipe. A 180degree image from the rear-view camera for reversing was by 2021 almost commonplace and if all that was not enough, "Rear Occupant Alert" could remind drivers

about to leave their children or pets in the back. It told them to check the back seats if the rear doors had been used at the start of a journey.

More premium features; a wireless charging pad for smartphones and a B&O Sound System with 10-speakers, an integrated subwoofer and a 575-watt Digital Signal Processing Amplifier to deliver selectable Surround Sound. The 21st century clientele was more computer-aware than their 1970s predecessors.

Fiestas were still on the B-car platform with a growing range of practical and refined

3-and 5-door variants with a taller bonnet and the blue oval badge within a larger grille. Trend and Titanium series featured a broad upper grille with horizontal strakes and a high gloss chrome surround with distinctive side vents. Titaniums had extra upper horizontal bars in hot-stamped chrome, matching the chrome window surrounds. Ford styling was supremely marketing-savvy.

Sporting character ST-Line Fiestas had an upper grille with deeper inset and gloss black honeycomb finish. The wide side vents were finished in body colour and a larger lower grille was added to imply raciness. They sprinted to 62mph (100 km/h) in 6.5 seconds, had a top speed of 143mph (230 kph) delivered by a 1.5 litre, providing 200 PS at 6,000 rpm and peak torque raised from 290 Nm to 320 Nm from 1,600 rpm to 4,000 rpm. Patented, cold-formed force vectoring springs and Tenneco twin-tube front dampers provided sharp turn-in and high levels of body control, while an optional Quaife mechanical limited-slip differential improved traction and cornering agility. There was even the option of a Track Mode that disabled traction control and set ESC to wide-slip mode for the growing popularity of amateur non-racing circuit driving.

In 2022 Ford announced Fiesta production would end in 2023. However, it was not quite the end of the Fiesta, going on to survive as a front runner in the used car markets of the world. It had shown good survival rates throughout its 40-odd years, its trade-in values were always well-sustained and now 21st century buyers were increasingly demanding not only good economy but also ecology-sensitive cars.

Grown-up long Fiesta Vignale.

PASSING ON
TO PUMA

Since 1967, when Ronald Reagan created the Californian Air Resources Board, legislators have been creating bans, limits and strictures. Spooked by climate emergencies and thoroughly well-intentioned, they made up their mind to outlaw cars with combustion engines. Green issues went to political heads, eventually leading to Low Emission Zones, Ultra-Low Emission Zones, bollarded No-Traffic Neighbourhoods and 20mph speed limits. Congestion charges raked in the cash.

In November 1991, California was demanding that by 2010 seven cars out of ten must be electric. The world became over-excited, convincing itself that it could invent batteries that would cope. Politicians anxious for green votes made promises that meant rewriting laws of physics and chemistry. There was progress in electric cars, but electricity is, ineluctably, only a means of transmitting power. It is not power.

Aware perhaps of what Ronald Reagan was planning in California in 1967, Ford in Britain brought out the Comuta. It demonstrated awareness of electric cars 40 years before the 21st century's environmental alarmism. Taking it seriously and accumulating engineering expertise was good for public relations; the ecology lobby was already lending weight, but most importantly the Comuta demonstrated what

Electric Ford 1. 1967 Comuta with Twiggy.

technology was up against in contemplating abandonment of internal combustion engines.

The Comuta was a convincing demonstration of how difficult it was to store sufficient energy in a self-contained automobile to provide enough range, performance, comfort and safety. And if Ford

Motor Company, with its huge resources, could not solve the electric car's problems, it looked as though mainstream battery-electric cars were still a long way off. Driving a Comuta was simple enough; it had an 'ignition' switch, a forwards and reverse lever, two pedals, a handbrake and a steering wheel, and whirred quietly into action… although not for long or very far.

It broke no new ground in the storage of electrical power and was not much better than a milk-float. There were plans to make the electric motors bigger, but it was not speed that was the problem as much as endurance. Ford's assistant managing director, Leonard Crossland, dismissed any hopes of putting the Comuta into production, although he tried to sound optimistic: "We expect electrical cars to be commercially feasible within the next 10 years, although we believe that they will be primarily city centre delivery vans and suburban shopping cars."

COMUTA 1967: 2-doors, 2+2-seats; weight 1200lb (544.3kg). 5bhp (3.7kW) @ 2000rpm; combined 81Nm (60lbft). 2 aircraft auxiliary series-wound DC electric motors 147mm (5.5in) dia; transversely mounted; thyristor control. Rear wheel drive; motors drive inwards through pinion to helical gear driving each rear wheel independently; no differential; final drive 4.05:1. Welded steel backbone chassis forming duct for interior heater; grp bodywork; ifs by forward-facing oblique arms on Neidhart rubber

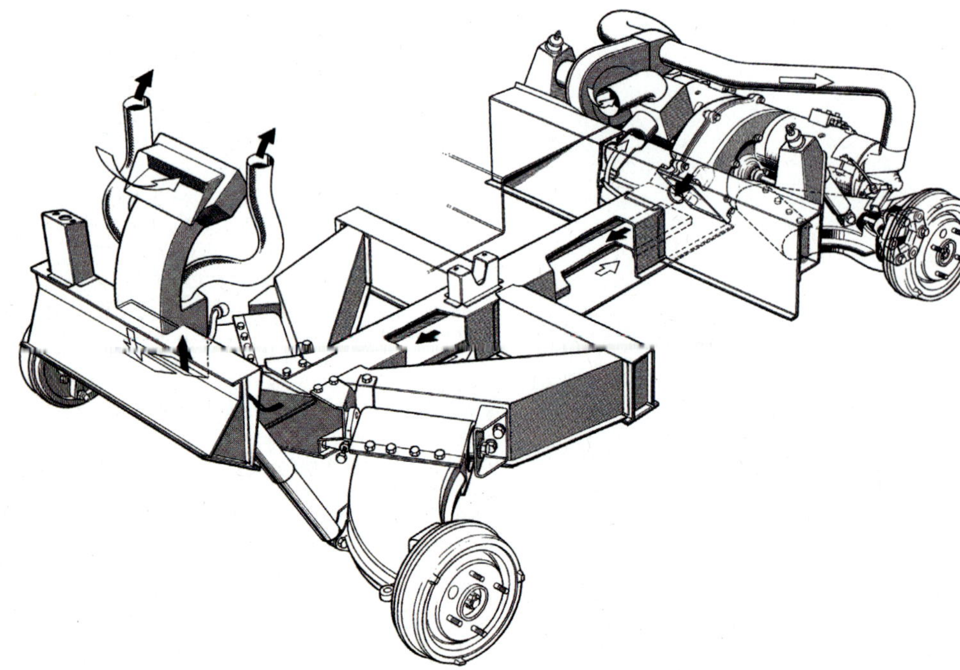

Basic box-section frame, electric engines, lead-acid batteries, milk-float technology.

Jenatzy drives in triumph. But not very far.

Hybrid alternative from GM, the Ampera.

Toyota Prius hybrid synergy drive 2009.

suspension bushes; IRS by trailing arms on Neidhart rubber suspension bushes; telescopic dampers; hydraulic drum brakes; 4 mid-mounted 12-volt 85-amp hour lead-acid batteries; 4.40 radial ply Goodyear tyres 10in wheels. Wheelbase 135.9cm (53.5in); track 111.8cm (44in); length 203.2cm (80in); width 125.7cm (49.5in); height 142.2cm (56in); turning circle 5.49m (18ft). Recirculating and fresh air interior heater. Max speed 64.2kph (40mph); 0-48kph (30mph) 12.5-14.0sec; 20.1kph (12.5mph) @ 1000rpm; range 64.4km (40 miles) at 40kph (25mph); restart gradient 1 in 5.

Battery capacity had improved since 1899 when Camille Jenatzy did 105.9 kph (66.8mph) with two direct drive 25kW motors (about 67bhp). Unfortunately, a flying kilometre at Achères was the limit for his 80-cell Fulmen accumulators, which had to be recharged before he could do an opposite-way kilometre for an official Land Speed Record. It was only a publicity stunt for Jenatzy's electric car factory and brought the Belgian a record but not a lot of luck. He died in a hunting mishap. Apparently something of a practical joker, Jenatzy hid in bushes making animal noises and somebody accidentally shot him.

In more recent times, the main challenges of battery capacity and weight have persisted. Electric cars may make a contribution to saving the planet, but concern about their high prices, limited range, short battery life and patchy recharging have remained. Batteries have always been heavy and bulky, with issues over their degradation. All electric cars gradually get slower as batteries age. There were worries over battery recycling, costs per kilowatt hour, and energy density. Recharging companies jostled to sell branded recharging volts while the Government's Net-Zero ambitions seemed not to consider less ecological alternatives such as battery-electric cars with engines to charge their own.

Claims for electric cars' range were challenged. Hilly journeys, high speeds or cold weather could reduce it by half. Estimates worked out on the Worldwide Harmonised Light Vehicle Test procedure, designed to simulate a mix of rural, urban and highway driving, invariably erred on the optimistic. Running an electric car was only cheap if you could charge it at home. Overnight household electricity cost about 10p per kWh; on the road you could pay up to 69p per kWh. Battery-electric cars cost 30 per cent more to buy and 30 per cent more to charge, and grants in the UK that had been worth £5000 in 2011 came down to £1500 in 2022 before being phased out altogether. Germany and France still made grants together with a bonus for scrapping an old petrol or diesel car. In the UK, electrics are expected to pay road tax from 2025 and a subsidy towards installing a home charging point has been withdrawn.

As for hybrids, using a combustion engine to charge vehicle batteries isn't a new idea. In 1933, the Fliegender Hamburger train ran the fastest timetabled service in the world – 77.4mph Berlin to Hamburg with two 810bhp V12 Maybachs driving Tatzlager electric traction motors. Diesel-electric submarines and gas turbine electric-hybrid buses, trucks and earthmovers were well-established. And the early 20th century saw Ferdinand Porsche proposing electric cars as well as planning a hybrid tank during the Second World War.

Perfectly good practical hybrids arrived with the new millennium. The Toyota Prius's official combined fuel consumption was 65.7mpg, although realistically it was only about 46mpg, which was good for the time. Its petrol engine was a basic 4-cylinder, inadequate for pushing a broad-shouldered saloon, so it had to work hard. General Motors' Vauxhall Ampera and others worked well and set a trend, although experience showed plug-in hybrids risked being run almost entirely on their combustion engines and hardly ever plugged in at all.

Hybrid cars defeated official greenhouse gas figures subtly, so nobody noticed at first. Their fuel consumption could be two-and-a-half to three times higher than bureaucrats thought. They could emit as much CO2 as petrol cars that didn't have burdensome batteries, and so a government plan to ban them (as well as pure ICE new cars) after 2035 was no surprise. One fleet user found drivers adopted hybrids for the right reasons but still consumed almost as much fuel as before, simply because they never went near a charging cable. The problem was not so much technology as the way legislation was framed. Official figures had been compiled on the basis that hybrid cars were plugged in to charging points and did not rely entirely on engines topping up the batteries.

There used to be a group of Fleet Street motoring correspondents. In 2009, its guest speaker, Dr Thomas Weber, responsible for Mercedes-Benz development, was spending €4.4 billion a year guessing what politicians would do next. Europe's leaders were becoming obsessed with climate change and safety, but he assured the group that industry would always find ways of making, selling and profiting from cars compliant with whatever rules governments made. If electric cars looked winsome, it would make them. If rules on diesel emissions were too strict, it would outflank them, which in due course it did.

Fiesta ST title winner.

Dr Weber was forced to admit it would all depend on second-guessing elected leaders, and that was impossible. He could not predict how far hydrogen fuel cell development would go, or whether petrol or diesel would be better for hybrids. It depended on matters over which neither he nor the rest of the motor industry had control. It could be legislation, infrastructure, energy prices, wars or whatever scare scientists came up with that week. He had a Plan A for some circumstances, Plan B for others, and a whole alphabet ready for whenever Brussels, London or California changed its collective mind.

He was sure of some things. Electric cars would be fine for towns (they always were) but not for dashing along the autobahn (they never were). He was sure combustion engines would shrink (they'd been getting smaller and more efficient for years) but beyond that we must wait and see. Whatever politicians subsidised, opposed, fostered or prohibited would determine the shape and specification of cars to come. Germany led the way in e-fuels, its transport minister Volker Wissing regarding them as essential for operating vehicles in a climate-neutral way. And Italy was critical of EU plans to ban engines, its transport minister stating that it made no sense and put jobs at risk.

Legislatures' wrangling showed how astute Ford's analysts had been. They had their own alphabet of plans but dared not admit them following obduracy encountered by electric car doubters, such as Akio Toyoda, president of Toyota. He had wondered if electric-only vehicles were the way ahead, joining a chorus of leaders, "… who can't speak out loudly." His way of addressing emissions problems was technology: "A silent majority is wondering whether EVs are really OK as a single option".

BMW-owned MINI said it had an all-electric model – but at the New York Motor Show, the company's global head, Oliver Zipse, was cautious. Mandating all vehicles to be pure electric, he said, had unintended consequences. People would hold on to their old higher-polluting cars rather than face the cost of electric ones. He was concerned about China's dominance in the supply of the materials essential for battery manufacture.

Carlos Tavares, CEO of Stellantis (which incorporates brands such as Fiat, Peugeot, Citroën, Vauxhall/Opel, Alfa Romeo, Chrysler and Jeep) said that a European ban would create social risk and alienate consumers with small budgets: "An electric car needs to drive 70,000 kilometres to compensate for the carbon footprint of manufacturing the battery. A small hybrid costs half as much as an EV."

Ford agreed with Mr Toyoda and, more than 50 years after its tentative Comuta, brought together its inspired 1.0-litre 3-cylinder engine and well-established Fiesta B-class underpinnings for its next new offering. The company stretched the platform by 14.6cm (9.5cm-plus on the wheelbase), as well as making it 7.1cm wider with a 5.8cm broader track. The roofline was higher, but with the engine taking up no more space than a sheet of foolscap paper, there was more room for people. The Issigonis Mini formula still rang true.

Autocar magazine was not alone in questioning the name of the ultimate Fiesta

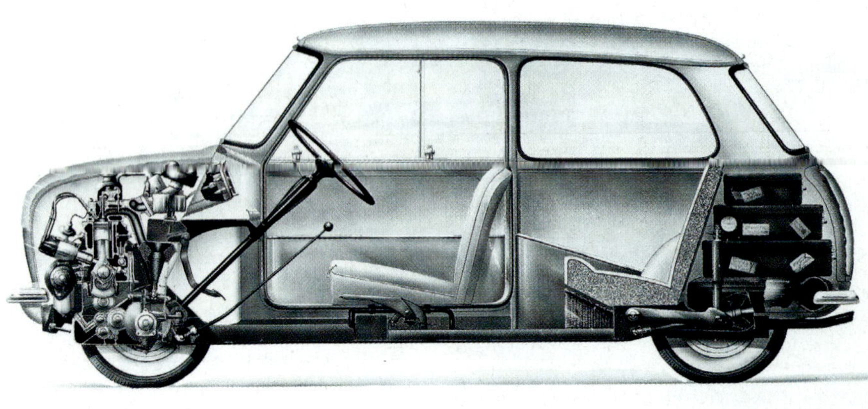

Derided Issigonis Mini formula, small engine, more space for people.

Born-again Fiesta. 2020 Puma ST.

replacement. "Since the Puma of the 1990s came with the tagline 'A driver's dream', Ford's decision to reprise the name of its pint-size coupé on the tailgate of a crossover seems perplexing. With a larger frontal area, a higher centre of gravity and more weight, this new Puma clearly distances itself from traditional 'driver's dream' territory where the 1034kg original did everything budgets would allow to get closer." However, it did show the difference between the new Puma and another Fiesta surrogate, wondering if it was no more than a cunning plan to make the Puma seem great by comparison with the unloved Ecosport.

The new Puma joined the rapidly growing crossover segment. On the basis that SUVs were based on the framework of something like a small truck or pick-up, anything with a car platform was a crossover, and there were now more compact crossovers than ever. Manufacturers were meeting the demand for volume while unusual, enthusiast-minded projects were diminishing. *Autocar* discovered that the new Puma filled a gap in the market for something genuinely good to drive: "It will slot into the range between the dreary Ecosport and the Kuga, and it shares a platform with Fiesta, which is easily the dynamic benchmark in the supermini class."

A 48V system encouraged its 3-cylinder petrol-turbo engine, which was available in both 123bhp and 153bhp guises. Mild hybrid assistance was an option for the 123bhp unit and standard on the 153bhp. All came with a 6-speed manual gearbox driving the front wheels. An integrated starter-generator replaced the alternator and, as well as recovering precious energy during braking, allowed the car to coast with the engine off while providing backfill torque. This improved throttle response and acceleration with a fairly modest boost of only 37lb.ft (27.6Nm). Driving a Puma, it was scarcely noticeable save for a facia display that told you.

The mild-hybrid system had another technical triumph. A cylinder deactivated itself like previous versions of the non-hybrid Ecoboost engine. Under light loads, the three cylinders cut down to just two within milliseconds, leaving the 15bhp, 37lb.ft electric motor to boost efficiency, performance, and flexibility. It pulled the car along from low revs impressively, as *Autocar* found: "Perhaps more important, it only allows you to become aware of the complexity of its operating brief in the most fleeting moments, sometimes with a hint of inconsistency in its braking response if you happen to knock the car out of gear early when decelerating, or with a slightly abrupt take-up of drive just as you tip into the accelerator pedal. These are problems you'd be likely to become conscious of only if you were anticipating them. Considering how much it plainly does to boost low-rev torque, saving you from otherwise necessary gearchanges, the mild-hybrid system adds much more to the car's overall drivability than it detracts."

Autocar was impressed with the end result: "On a wet test day, it took a two-way average of 10 seconds to hit 60mph from rest, a fairly strong if not exceptional showing. But the fact that it was almost 7 seconds (or about 40%) quicker accelerating from 30mph to 70mph in fourth gear than the

Puma. Small engine, small space.

Above: Red Bull livery for Puma hybrid rally car. Main image: Sebastien Loeb and Isabelle Galmiche: Monte Carlo Rally with Puma hybrid.

1.0-litre turbocharged Nissan Juke illustrates the difference made by this hybrid system. When pulling from low engine speeds in higher gears, you can feel the torque it contributes quite clearly – and, if you watch the tacho needle, you can also feel the point in the rev range (just above 4000rpm) when the electric motor has to switch off."

Meanwhile, the same magazine test offered advice for any would-be Puma owner: "The car has a healthy-feeling outright performance level for mixed road driving and a short, pleasant, well-defined gearshift action. It's smooth enough and as powerful and stable as it needs to be under braking, although it's easier to judge your initial pedal inputs once you've learned to squeeze the middle pedal only after you've already selected a lower gear. It's best not to downshift in the middle of a deceleration phase where you can avoid it, since doing so interferes slightly with the regenerative braking you get from the hybrid system and spoils the initial braking response a little."

One Ford designer cheerfully described the Puma's shape as 'anti-wedge', intended to steal sales from premium brands, notably BMW's Mini. The Puma offered one of the largest load areas in its class and more passenger space than a Fiesta, although the mild-hybrid's additional battery dropped outright space from 456 to 401 litres with the rear seats in place. Under the boot floor, however, was the 80-litre Megabox, a hard plastic container for carrying muddy boots or wet raincoats with a plug in the floor so it could be rinsed out and drained.

Compared with the outgoing Fiesta, the Puma felt more supple, with a stiffer rear torsion beam and firmer suspension bushes with new top mounts. Some crossovers had firm springing as a result of a taller body affecting cornering. *Autocar* found that when the Puma's electronic traction and stability controls did intervene, they did it progressively and without intruding on the driver. There was an option to disable the traction control, leaving the stability aid on in any circumstances: "Just occasionally, once you've really got to grips with the potential of the chassis and are at risk of actually enjoying yourself, that does seem a shame

Scottish Car of the Year with ASMW president Jack McKeown at Dundee awards.

2022
90e
2022
RALLYE MONTE-CARLO
WRC
FiA WORLD RALLY CHAMPIONSHIP
#RallyeMonteCarlo
LE CASINO
MONTE·CARLO
LA BOUTIQUE OFFICIELLE
france bleu
acm.mc
Red Bull
Ford
SafetyCulture
Castrol
Asahi KASEI
FORD PERFORMANCE
Powered by ECOBOOST HYBRID

Puma tailpiece.

when it begins to intrude on the car's ability to entertain."

Even entry-level Titanium Pumas came with autonomous emergency braking, conventional cruise control and lane-keeping assist. An optional £900 Driver Assistance pack brought blind spot warning, cross-traffic alert and traffic jam assist systems, among others, and added 'intelligent' distance-keeping to the cruise control. *Autocar* reported: "The systems are generally tuned so as to be quite discreet but can, in most cases, be adjusted for sensitivity and, in some cases, deactivated completely. Even in its most sensitive setting, the lane-keeping aid keeps the driver engaged. However, it didn't always detect the bounds of a motorway lane through roadworks or in bad weather."

Ford was not as adventurous with the Puma's interior as it was with its bold lines, wide grille and flat waistline. It was well-proportioned, but there wasn't much in its cabin to separate it from any other Ford; finished in darker shades of cloth and a mix of soft and hard plastics, it was almost drab. Trim levels were Titanium at the entry level, followed by ST-Line and ST-Line X.

An M-Sport Puma Hybrid Rally1 took part in the 2022 Monte Carlo Rally. Ford's first electrified competition car's hybrid powertrain captured energy during braking and coasting, storing it in the 3.9kWh battery, supplementing the turbocharged 1.6-litre EcoBoost petrol engine from its 100kW electric motor. It went through towns and cities using electric-only, charging the battery pack at service points between stages. Ott Tänak and Martin Jarveoja claimed their first victory with M-Sport Ford World Rally Team and the Ford Puma Hybrid Rally1 in 2023 after an exemplary drive in Sweden on only his second FIA World Rally Championship outing in the car. Tänak claimed his second Rally Sweden victory and his first win with M-Sport since 2017.

Ford's announcement that it was abandoning the Fiesta was not entirely true. It was really only abandoning the Fiesta title. The Puma was essentially a continuity Fiesta made elsewhere, and its removal from its regular production centres was consequential to Ford's share price. One columnist questioned the explanation given by Tim Slatter, chairman of Ford in Britain, for cutting 1300 jobs in the UK, 1000 of them in product development that accompanied the Fiesta's end. The company's claim to be moving towards a wholly electric fleet by the end of the decade looked like PR spin and avoided any commitment to what Slatter's claim of going "wholly electric" really meant.

The Spectator was among those scornful of Ford seeming to abandon the mass market and withdrawing from petrol and diesel. If loyal customers could no longer buy sub-£20,000 Fiestas, they seemed unlikely to switch to £50,000-£60,000 electric crossovers and SUVs from Ford, potentially opting for cheaper Chinese alternatives instead. Ford global profits fell unexpectedly in the 4th quarter of 2022 and sales were 100,000 down.

It seemed unthinkable not to have a Ford in the UK's top three, but it was now no higher than 7th with the Puma, while the Fiesta was down to 10th. Yet as many world car makers were privately, sometimes even publicly admitting, battery-electric cars were reaching their peak. It was, alas, Public Relations suicide to say so. Ford claimed it wanted to reinvent itself as a more upmarket, all-electric brand, given the Net-Zero commitment to ban sales of new petrol and diesel cars from 2030 and hybrids from 2035. By 2023 hybrid sales were almost matching battery electric. Nearly six cars in ten sold in Britain were petrol, fewer than 8 in 100 diesel. Hybrids were rising to 14 per cent while pure electrics slowed.

More than a decade ago, Ford's engineers invented one of the cleverest 3-cylinder turbocharged engines ever put into a production car. Ford may keep claiming it would like to go fully electric, yet the Fiesta's successor, the Puma, is a perectly formed hybrid and a far better reply to battery-elecrtic optimists. *(Ford)*

BUYING A CLASSIC
FIESTA

The first four generations of Fiesta have evolved into collectable cars on today's classic market. If you're tempted to jump on board, what should you be checking for?

From the numerous generations of Fiesta built for Europe during a phenomenal 47-year career, the first four are now firmly ensconced in the classic car scene, with a loyal following in each case. From the earliest MkI of 1976 through to the last of the MkIVs built just prior to the new millennium, these classic Fiestas offer a range of attributes – with a version available to suit most budgets and tastes.

From economical runabouts to strong-performing hot hatches, these are the Fiestas that fans of classic and retro cars now seek out. And with prices ranging from just a few hundred pounds for a late-model car in need of cosmetic attention through to five-figure sums for sought-after sporting versions, just about every potential buyer is catered for. But what needs checking before you take the classic Fiesta plunge?

MkI & MkII BUYING

The similarities between the MkI and MkII Fiesta are such that the buying experience is essentially the same, with the second-generation version being simply a lightly restyled and mildly upgraded version of the original. Both, of course, were huge success, particularly in the UK where the Fiesta was a seemingly permanent Top 5 contender. It was Britain's bestselling supermini as early as 1978, and just two years later more than a million had found homes throughout Europe.

The Fiesta MkI employed the well-proven Kent crossflow engine in upgraded Valencia guise featuring a shorter block, closer bores and a three-bearing crank. Capacities of 957cc and 1117cc were initially offered, although a modified version of the five-bearing Kent crossflow subsequently made its way into the Fiesta in 1298cc guise for the range-topping Ghia and S.

Throughout the MkI's production run, the versions available comprised 'Base', Popular, Popular Plus, L, GL, Ghia, S, Supersport and XR2, plus a list of limited editions that included the Kingfisher, Sandpiper, Firefly, Festival, Bravo, Quartz and Finesse. The Supersport of 1980 was based around the 1300 Sport but featured extras from the Series-X accessories catalogue. For 1981, the basic Fiesta was dropped in favour of Popular and Popular Plus versions, with the whole range facelifted soon after to feature bigger bumpers and interior upgrades. Also in 1981 came the sporty XR2, using a tweaked version of the 1598cc Kent engine, round headlights and uprated sports suspension.

The MkII Fiesta debuted in 1983, using essentially the same bodyshell but with a more curvaceous front end that provided space for the 1297cc CVH engine from the Escort, plus its five-speed gearbox. The smaller OHV engines remained, and for the first time there was a 1.6-litre diesel. The MkII

The XR2 added sportiness to the Fiesta line-up in 1984.

XR2 arrived in 1984 offering an extra 12bhp over its predecessor thanks to its use of the 1596cc CVH engine from the Escort XR3. Later changes included the 1.3 engine being replaced by a 1.4-litre lean burn unit, also fitted to the 1.4 S launched in 1986. The MkII finally ceased production in early 1989.

For today's MkI or MkII buyers, the biggest concern is bodywork, with the front wings and front panel (particularly the seam between them), the windscreen scuttle, the bottoms of the doors, the rear valance and around the fuel filler being particularly susceptible to rust. Rear wheelarches are also prone to corrosion,

with the XR2's plastic body kit often hiding rot. And you should be on the look-out for structural rust around the front strut mounts as well as in the bulkhead, inner wings and boot floor, plus the sills, outer edges of the front footwells and 'chassis' rails.

Various panels and repair sections – including inner and outer sills, wings, front panels, rear arches, rear panels and various repair sections – are available from Magnum Panels (magnumcarpanels.co.uk). Ex-Pressed Steel Panels (steelpanels.co.uk) also offers a range of Fiesta items, including sills, A-posts, battery trays, floorpans and boot floors.

When it comes to engines, the Valencia is reliable when maintained properly but you should check for signs of wear, including blue smoke, high oil consumption and a rough tickover; timing chain rattle isn't usually an issue, but any 'clacking' from the top end can be a sign of broken camshaft followers. The Kent crossflow is also strong but can suffer from a noisy valvetrain as well as piston and bore wear when neglected. As for the CVH, a noisy top end can mean that the camshaft is damaged due to the lifters being sludged

up because of infrequently changed oil, while poor running is often caused by a worn distributor that's advancing too early.

Most MkI/MkII Fiestas come with a four-speed BC gearbox, with some later cars featuring the five-speed BC5. Any rumbling sounds suggest the differential bearings have collapsed, which can only be solved with a rebuild. Any difficulty in selecting gears is usually down to wear in the linkage, while high mileage cars can suffer from synchromesh wear.

In terms of running gear, wear in the rear trailing arms is a common MoT fail (check for any clunking from the rear). Worn dampers and springs are cheap and easy to replace, while changing the track control arms and tie bar bushes can transform the car's steering response. Any braking problems are likely to be a simple fix, although an inefficient handbrake can be tricky to adjust thanks to the complex pulley mechanism. If you can feel a vibration when braking, the front discs are likely to be warped – but don't worry too much as new discs are inexpensive, as are wheel cylinders, rear brake shoes and even brake calipers.

New-old-stock trim for both the MkI and MkII Fiesta is rare now, so be extra vigilant when checking the interior. The top of the back seat is prone to sun damage, while the vinyl seats of basic models tend to crack and fabric ones go baggy. Cracked dashboards are common (mostly on the MkI), while parcel shelves without holes cut for speakers can command a premium. Check for any dampness inside the car (a possible sign of floor or bulkhead corrosion), and check that the electrics are all in working order.

MkIII & MkIV BUYING
The launch of the Fiesta MkIII in April 1989 marked the first major redesign of a model that had been a bestseller for almost 13 years. In came a completely new platform, with a wheelbase six inches longer than before, together with much-improved suspension. The extra length enabled the Fiesta to finally grow up, with 5-door versions joining the 3-door models to put Ford's

The MkII was appealing to young insurance conscious drivers.

The third incarnation of the Fiesta grew in size, offering buyers more engine, door number and interior choices.

supermini on an equal footing with the Fiat Uno and Peugeot 205.

Low-spec versions used 1.0- and 1.1-litre engines, with 1.4- and 1.6-litre CVH units offered further up the range. The XR2i's 1.6 CVH came with electronic fuel-injection and a colour-coded body kit, joined in 1990 by what many fans consider the ultimate MkIII Fiesta: the 129mph RS Turbo. Ford finally introduced its Zetec 16-valve engine in 1992, powering the later XR2i and RS1800, while the less powerful but still sporty 1.4 Si joined the range later.

The MkIII was updated in 1994 via a stiffer bodyshell, side-impact beams and revised suspension. But more extensive changes came with the MkIV Fiesta of October 1995, which featured trim upgrades (including a new-look front end complete with oval-shaped grille) and a Yamaha-developed Zetec-SE powerplant in 1.25- or 1.4-litre form. Meanwhile, the Fiesta Mk3 continued as the entry-level Fiesta Classic until 1997, plus the badge-engineered Mazda 121. The MkIV was replaced by the heavily revised MkV in October 1999.

As with earlier Fiestas, rust is the biggest problem facing today's buyers. Cosmetic corrosion can often be found around the rear wheelarches, rear quarters, front wings, tailgate and door frames, particularly under the rubber seals. The bodywork around the MkIII's fuel cap can also rust spectacularly. And you should also check carefully the battery tray, inner wings, bulkhead and front crossmember, as well as the A-pillars and inner/outer sills and front floorpan. You should also check for damp carpets, as well as for rust in the boot floor, rear suspension turrets and outer valance. Body panels are available, but it's only on XR or RS versions that any extensive restoration will make financial sense.

Many MkIIIs feature a derivate of the old Valencia engine in 999cc, 1118cc or 1297cc forms. It's not particularly refined and can suffer from wear and neglect; check for excessive smoke, oil leaks and knocking from the bottom end; valve stem oil seals and piston rings are common problem areas. CVH engines, meanwhile, were used in 1392cc and 1596cc forms, the latter in carb-fed, fuel-injected and turbocharged set-ups; noisy tappets and camshaft rattling is typical, but listen for heavier growling from the crank, and check it's not breathing from the oil filler. If the cambelt hasn't been replaced recently, you need to factor this in to your budget.

Zetec and Zetec SE-engined machines are quieter and more refined, as well as capable of very high mileages without issue as long as oil changes and cambelt swaps are made regularly. You should walk away if there's blue exhaust smoke or the bottom end is overly noisy; if there's stalling, erratic idling or fluctuating revs, this could be down to problems with the sensors, idle speed control valve or coil pack.

As with the previous Fiestas, the MkIII used BC four-speed and BC5 five-speed transmissions, while the five-speed in the MkIV was an upgraded unit known as iB5. All are reliable, but any wear is likely to be felt via general sloppiness (which could suggest a

The 1990 Fiesta Bonus.

The Fiesta Si came with 'bubble' bumpers and metallic green paint.

worn linkage) or difficulty in selecting gears, the latter possibly due to broken teeth on the BC5's clutch self-adjusting ratchet. Check for 'slip' when pulling away too, as clutch failure isn't uncommon.

As you might expect, these generations of Fiesta continued the tradition of relatively simple and robust running gear, although the best-handling cars are undoubtedly the later MkIIIs and subsequent MkIVs. In fact, so impressive was the MkIV's handling and roadholding, its platform formed the basis of the sporty Puma coupe. Biggest problems are likely to be tired springs and dampers (check for general 'looseness' on your test drive), while worn bushes or track rod ends can cause wandering, as can a steering rack in need of replacement. Listen for any clonking from the front (probably caused by broken drop links or lower suspension arms), as well as any rumbling from the wheel bearings.

MkIII and MkIV brakes are a simple design and easy to work on, with parts also being reassuringly inexpensive. If there's any juddering through the pedal when you're braking, it could be a sign of warped or worn discs, or potentially a sticking caliper (especially if the car pulls to one side). It's not unusual for rear drums to stop working on the handbrake mechanism, while sticking rear bias valves can cause uneven braking. If your MkIV is a high-spec model fitted with ABS, check that it's working as it should; you should also make sure the dashboard ABS light comes on with the ignition and goes off again once the car's running.

Advantages of the MkIII/MkIV over earlier Fiestas include their more spacious interiors, which were also finished to a slightly higher standard. With the youngest cars having been around for almost a quarter of a century, however, you obviously need to be on the look-out for wear and tear as well as signs of abuse. Even though quality was well up to class standards of the '90s, you can expect to find dashboard rattles and sagging seats and door cards on well-used cars. Original trim will be hard to find, but there are still plenty of MkIII and MkIV Fiestas being scrapped or broken for spares, so finding secondhand replacement items shouldn't be too difficult.

You'll need to make sure that electrical items are all in working order, particularly on top-spec cars fitted with electric windows and so on. It's not unusual for the central locking and boot release mechanisms to fail, and you should make sure that the heater is working and the temperature can still be adjusted. Electrical problems aren't uncommon, but are often caused by nothing more serious than a corroded connector or bad earth.

TODAY'S VALUES

What's notable about the first four generations of Fiesta on today's classic car market is the broad spread of values, meaning there's a version available to suit most budgets. Admittedly, fans of the MkI can no longer pick up their favourite car for just a few hundred pounds (those days are long gone), but switching their search to a MkIII or MkIV can yield a real bargain, particularly if you're happy to consider a car needing work.

The updated MkIV Fiesta, with its chrome oval grill.

MkI and MkII XR2s have followed the trend of all things 80s going up dramatically in value.

Values of MkIs and MkIIs have risen dramatically over the past decade, although they seem more stable now. If you crave a low-mileage MkI XR2 in exceptional condition, you can pay up to £20,000, while examples that are useable but in need of some minor cosmetic improvement can be found for less than half that amount. Budget £12,000-£15,000 and you should be able to pick up a MkI XR2 in excellent order, with rarities like the 1300S and Supersport being not far behind. A MkII XR2 will be more affordable, aided by its longer production run.

Standard MkI and MkII Fiestas are, of course, much lower in value, with excellent examples available for £3500-£5000 depending on their spec level, mileage and overall condition, while cars needing a few cosmetic improvements can be found from around £2000-£2500 and projects from £1000 or so.

The MkIII and MkIV models, however, really do buck today's trend for high-value old Fords, with even the sportiest models costing much less to buy than their MkI and MkII predecessors. An XR2i, for example, can be bought for £5000-£6000 in good order, while the RS Turbo sporting flagship isn't hugely more expensive, coming in at not much more than half the price of its equivalent Escort. Meanwhile, for anyone willing to consider a non-sporty MkIII or MkIV, this is where the real bargains can be found, with project cars available for little more than scrap money, and MoT'd and useable examples from as little as £1000 (or sometimes less). Around £1500-£1800 should buy you a tidy survivor in Ghia spec, while even low-mileage survivors in superb condition are unlikely to exceed £2500 in today's market.

OUR VERDICT

Taking the Fiesta through the first half of its lengthy career were the MkI to MkIV models that now offer classic car fans a wide array of attributes, with a version to suit all tastes. For anyone considering their first classic, a Fiesta makes a particularly good choice – just as it did among first-time buyers when it was new. Whether you're buying a high-value MkI XR2 or a cheap and cheerful base-model MkIV, you'll find it pleasing to drive, simple to work on and economical to run.

With affordable parts prices and a simple spec in its favour, the classic Fiesta also makes a sound choice for any DIY-minded buyers who fancy taking on a project. Just make sure you don't underestimate the amount of work needed, as it's all too easy for restoration costs to exceed the end value of a non-sporting derivative.

The sporting MkIII Fiesta's represent fantastic value for classic Ford hot-hatches.